The
DISAPPEARING PUMPKIN CHOIR

Photos & Stories

CATHRYN WELLNER

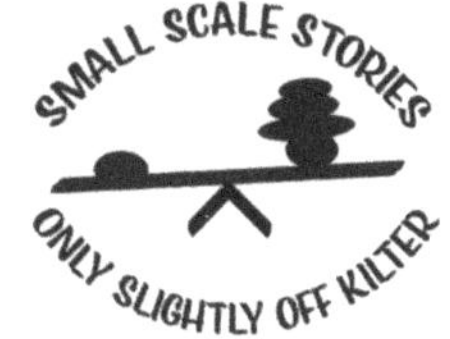

Small Scale Stories #3
Espoir Press
British Columbia 2017

Espoir Press
1002 - 1128 Sunset Drive
Kelowna, British Columbia
Canada V1Y 9W7

The Disappearing Pumpkin Choir (Small Scale Stories #3)

ISBN 978-1-988760-04-9

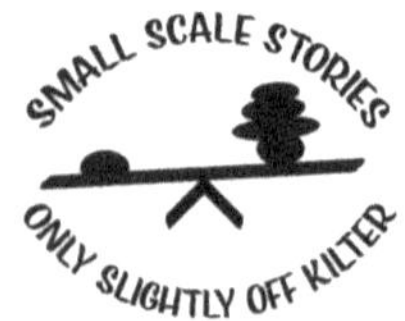

INTRODUCTION

Night falls. Quiet reigns in the neighborhood. Around three in the morning chaos breaks loose. I used to figure the honking Canada geese were waking in the night, arguing over the best sleep spots. Now I think maybe the adolescents wing in after partying into the wee hours and are met by scolding adults.

A little further away, the Japanese garden closes its gates for the night. We humans are in awe of the beauty that lies within the surrounding fence. But what if things change at night? What if the serene crabapple trees and sunny forsythia cut loose? What if they let their leaves down and tell jokes too scandalous for human ears?

Even without being allowed into the secret world of the plants, animals and supposedly inanimate objects around us, we can see Nature's sense of fun. She carves faces into stones, gives crows raucous songs, makes tree roots strong enough to obliterate sidewalks, and offers clouds the entire sky for playing shape games.

We humans are invited to the party. Join the celebration in this third book of Small Scale Stories. They are only Slightly Off Kilter.

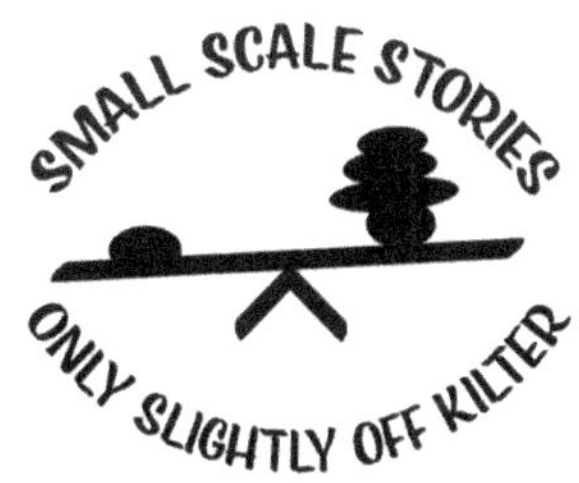

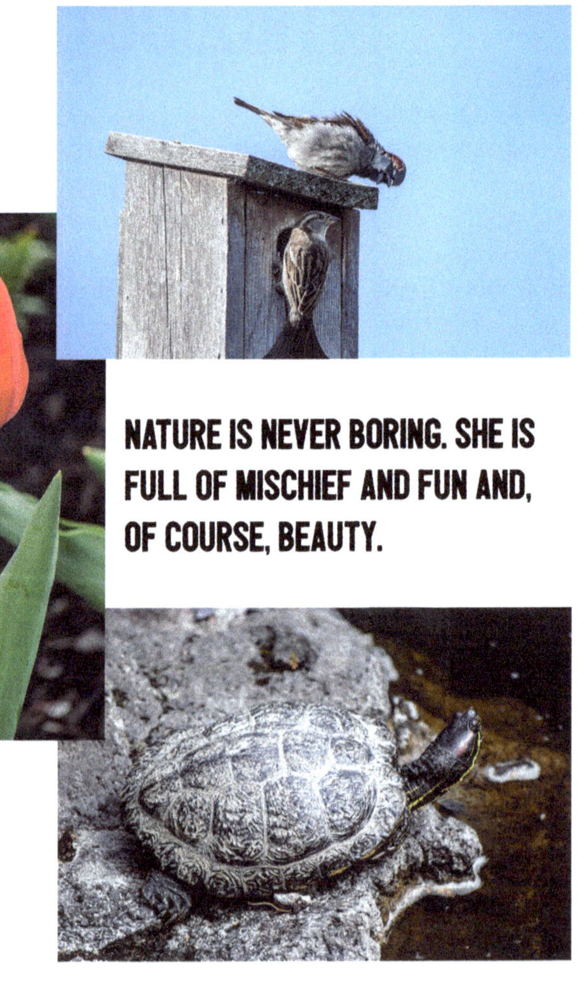

NATURE IS NEVER BORING. SHE IS
FULL OF MISCHIEF AND FUN AND,
OF COURSE, BEAUTY.

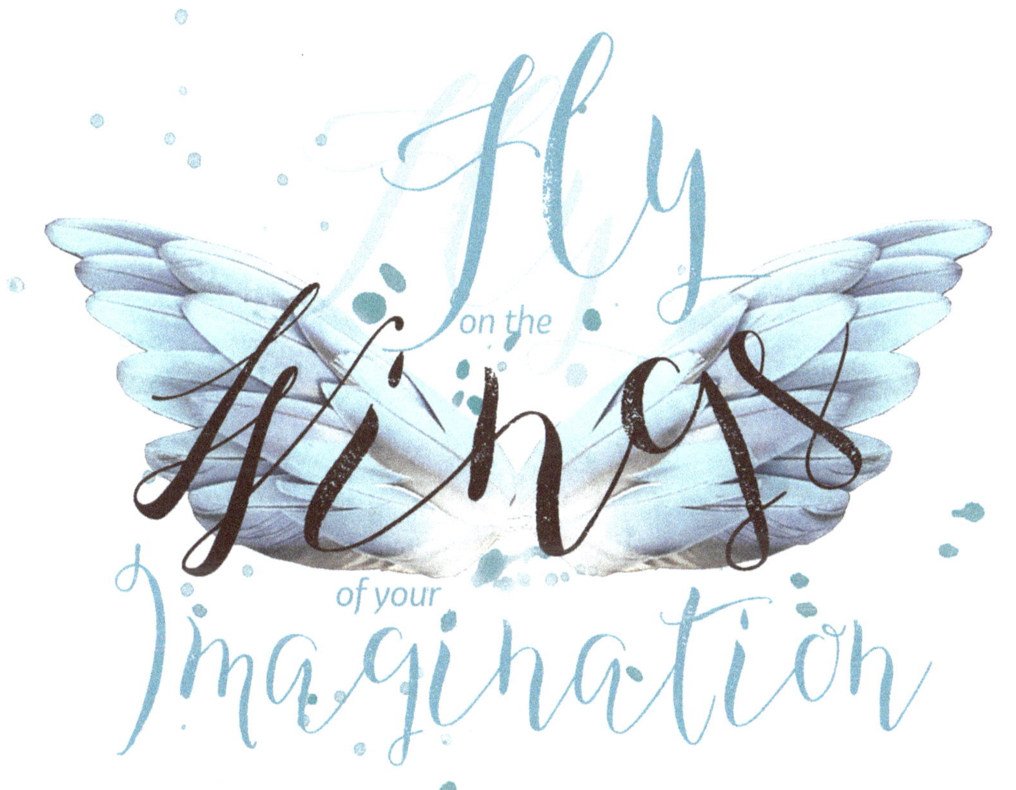

Fly
on the
wings
of your
Imagination

THE STORIES

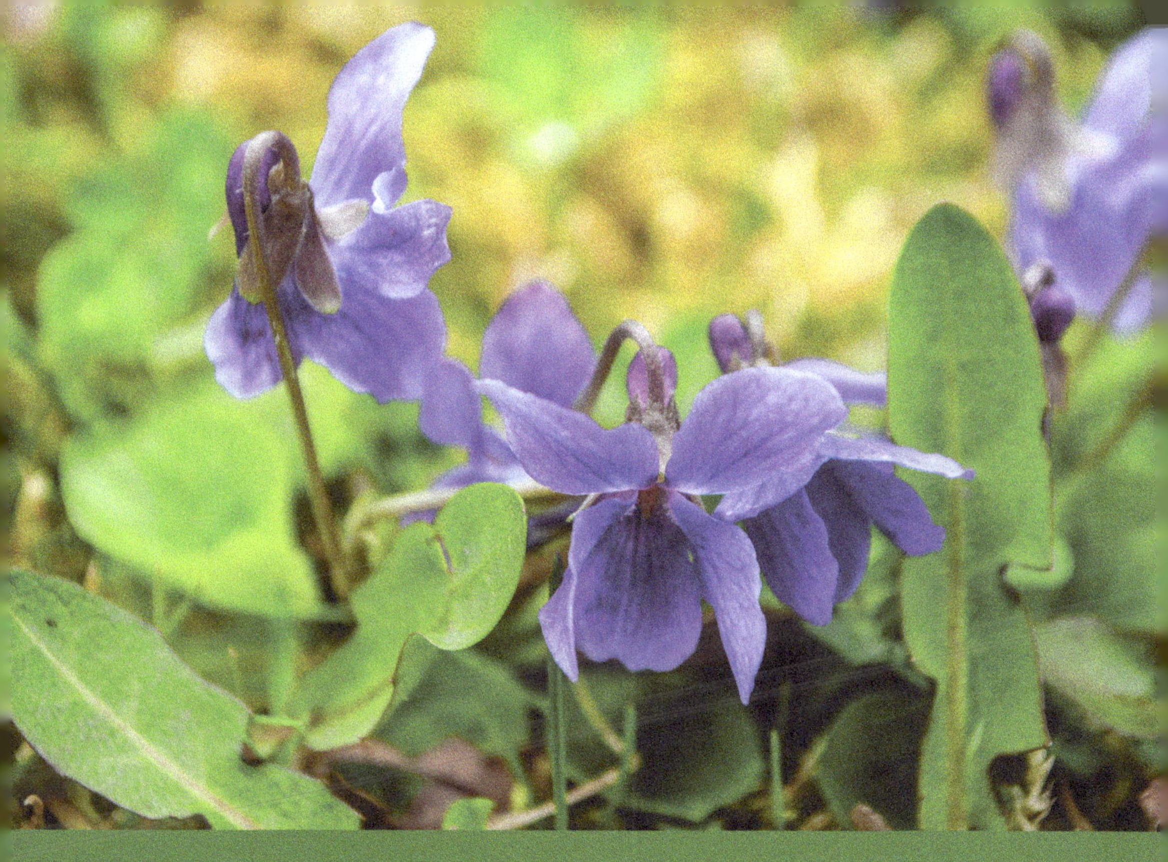

After weeks of rain, people feared spring would never come. Violets knew how to be patient but decided to give the humans a reassuring boost.

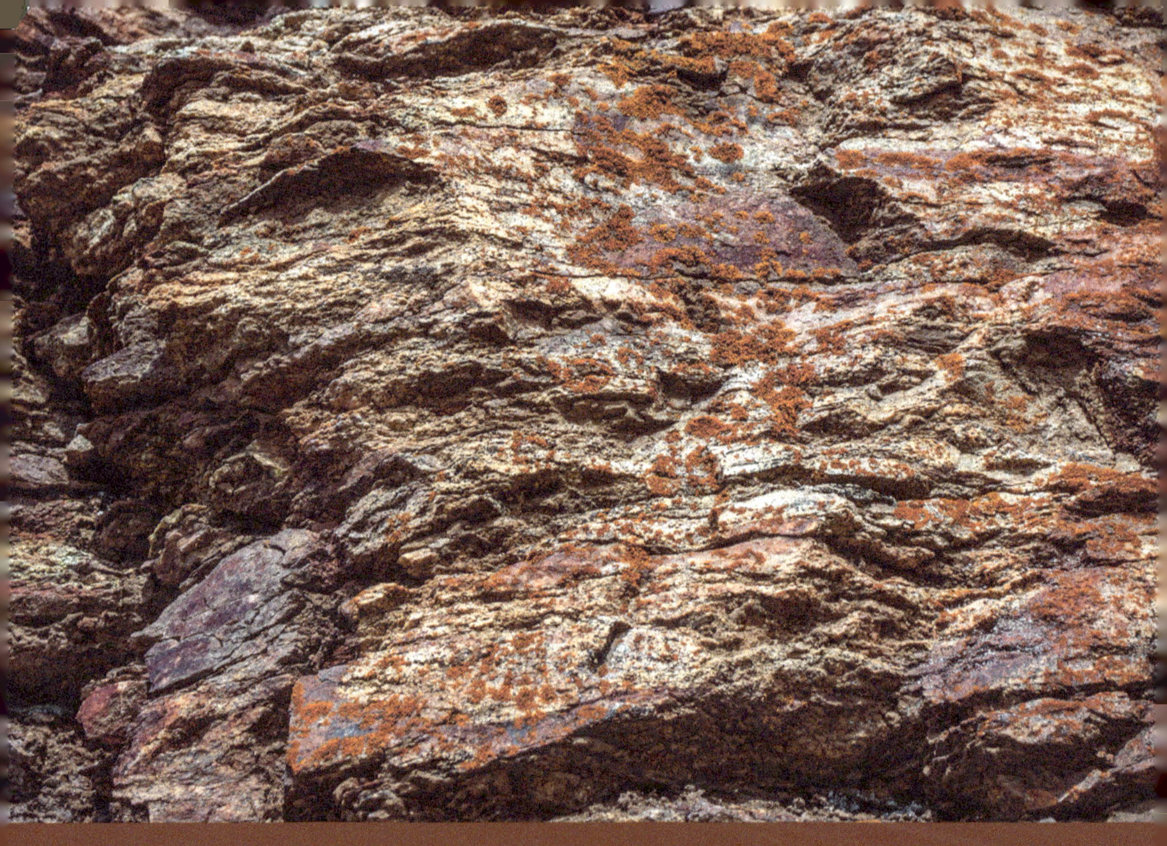

He listened to the hikers passing by, wondering when someone would notice how much his lined face and mossy beard made him look like Abraham Lincoln.

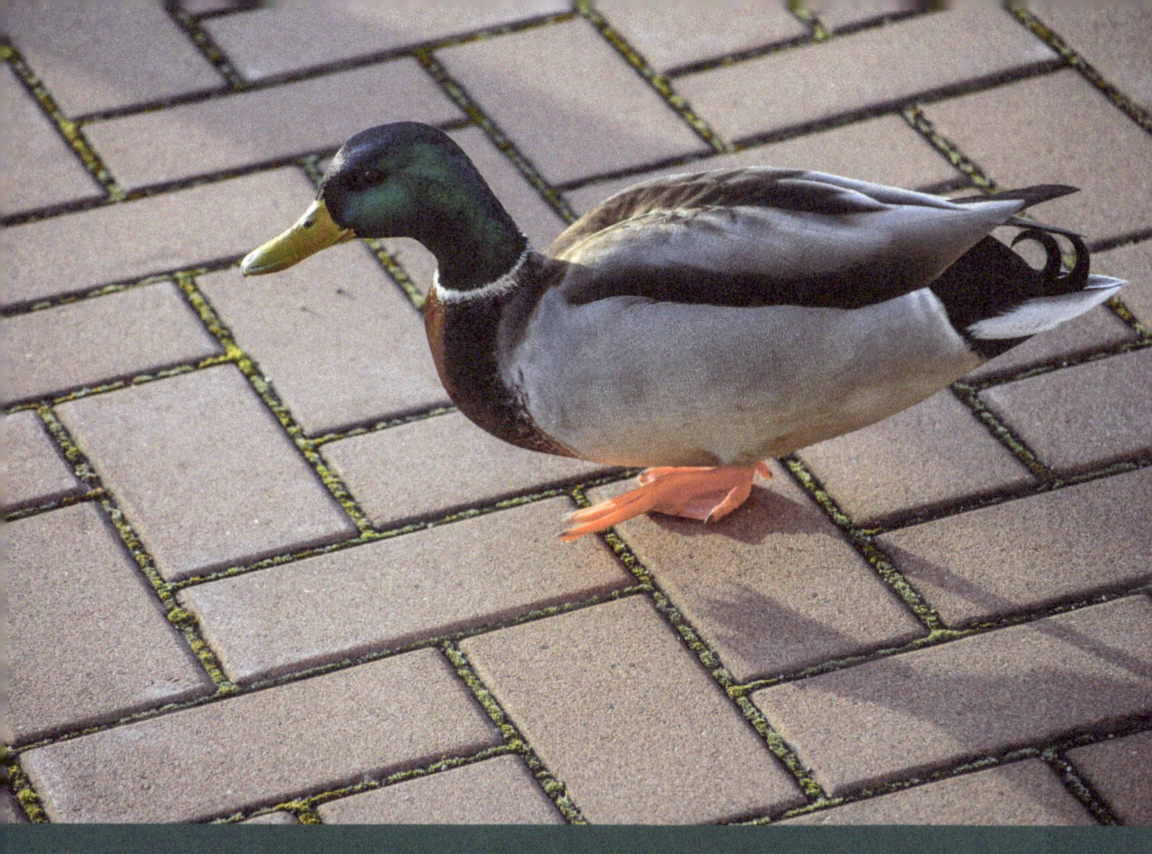

"One, two, cha, cha, cha." Mallard knew the humans had no idea he was imitating their dance. He hoped they would practice outside again. He understood the basics but not that crazy turn step.

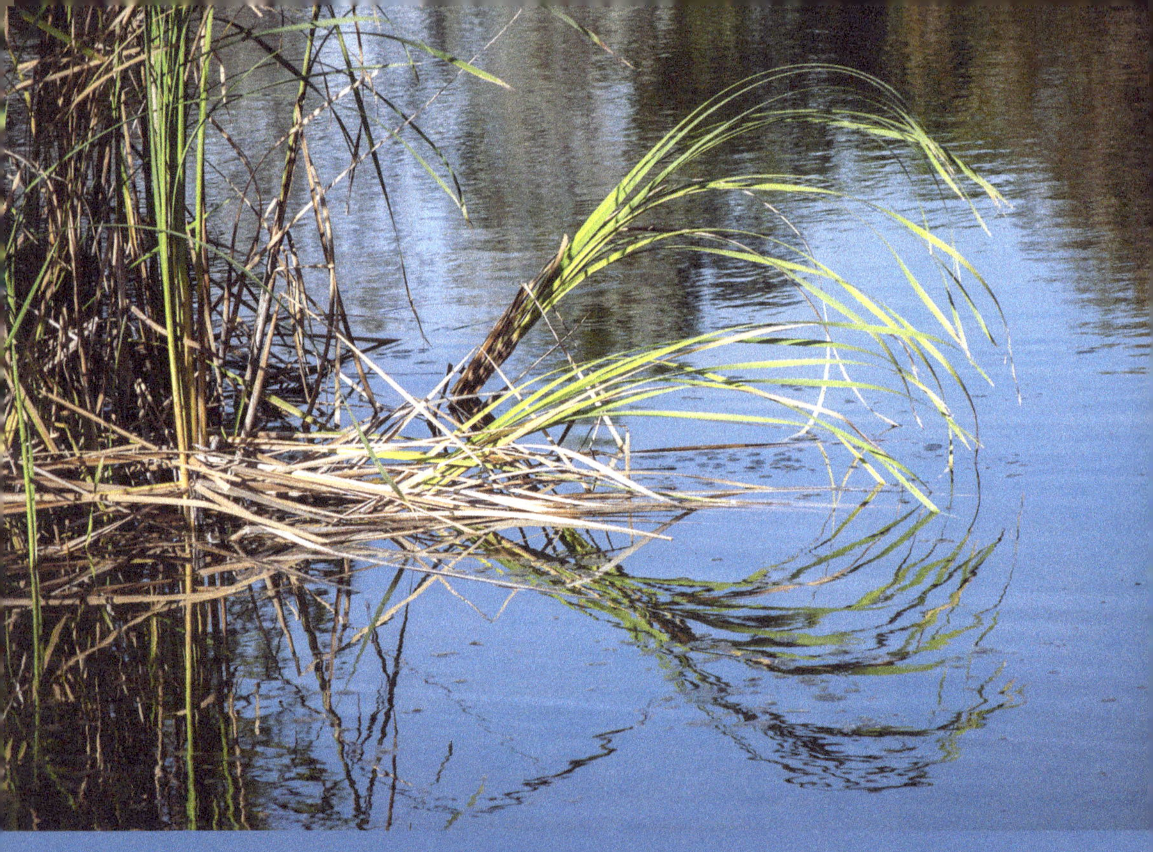

The upright neighbors laughed when a deer knocked the reeds askew. They were soon envious when they saw the leaning reeds play Beware the Green-Claw Monster with their friend, the pond.

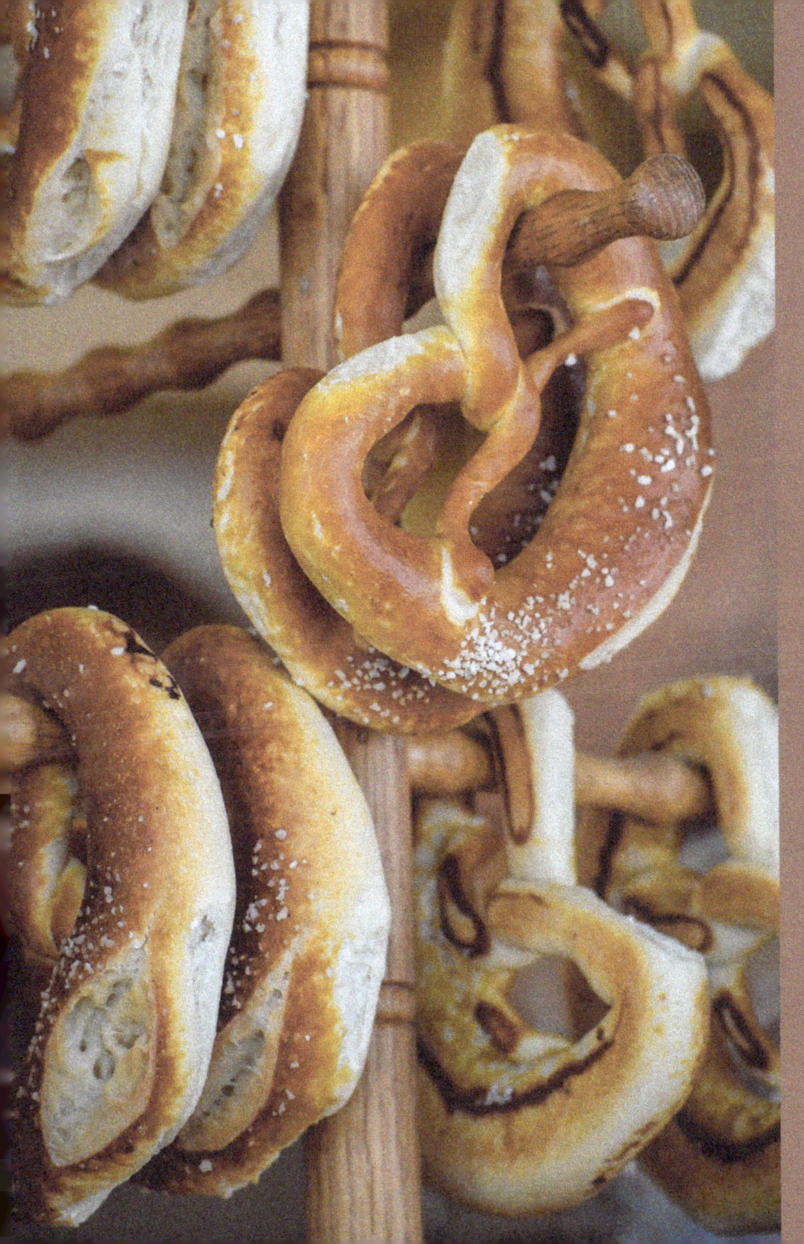

The pretzels perked up when they heard people exclaim how yummy they looked. They were too young to know the fate that was in store for them.

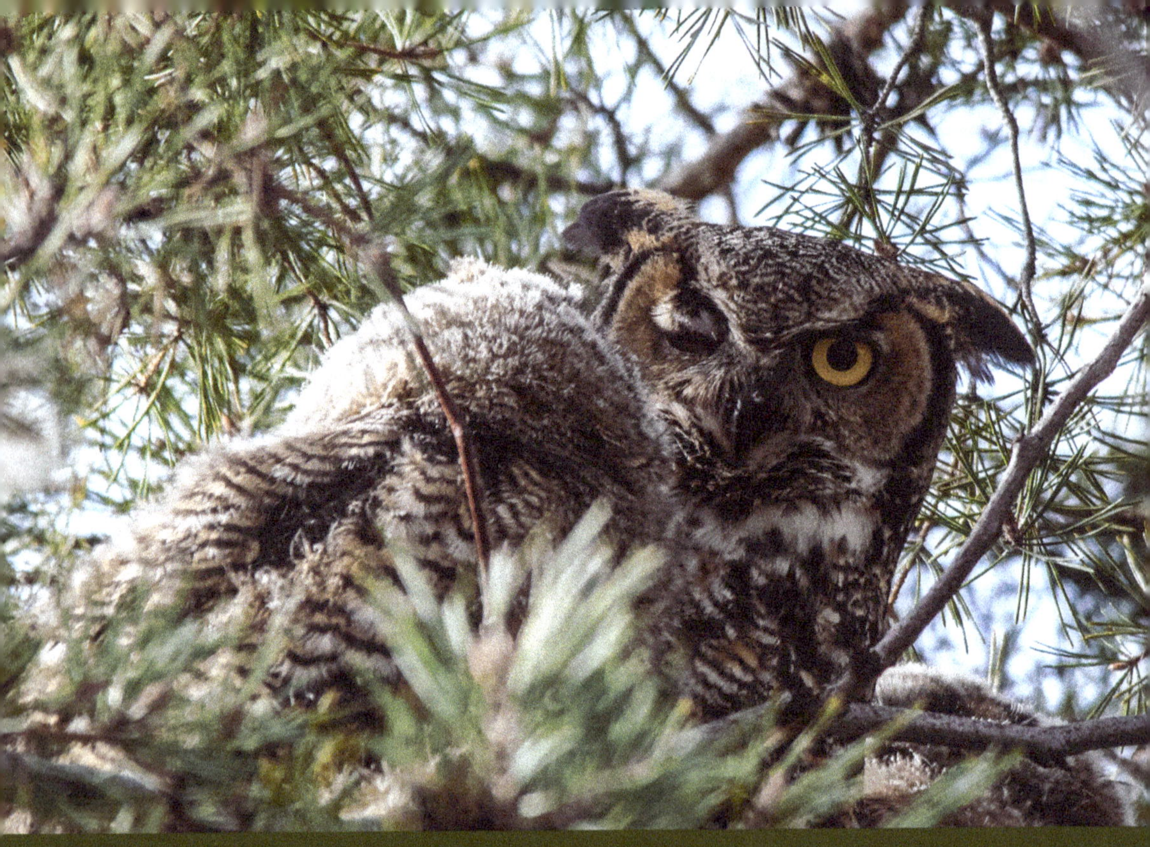

"Long, long ago, in a tree far away, there lived a brave Great-Horned Owl." Owlet sighed. Dad had told her the story many times. She wondered if it was his way of encouraging her to master flight and leave the nest.

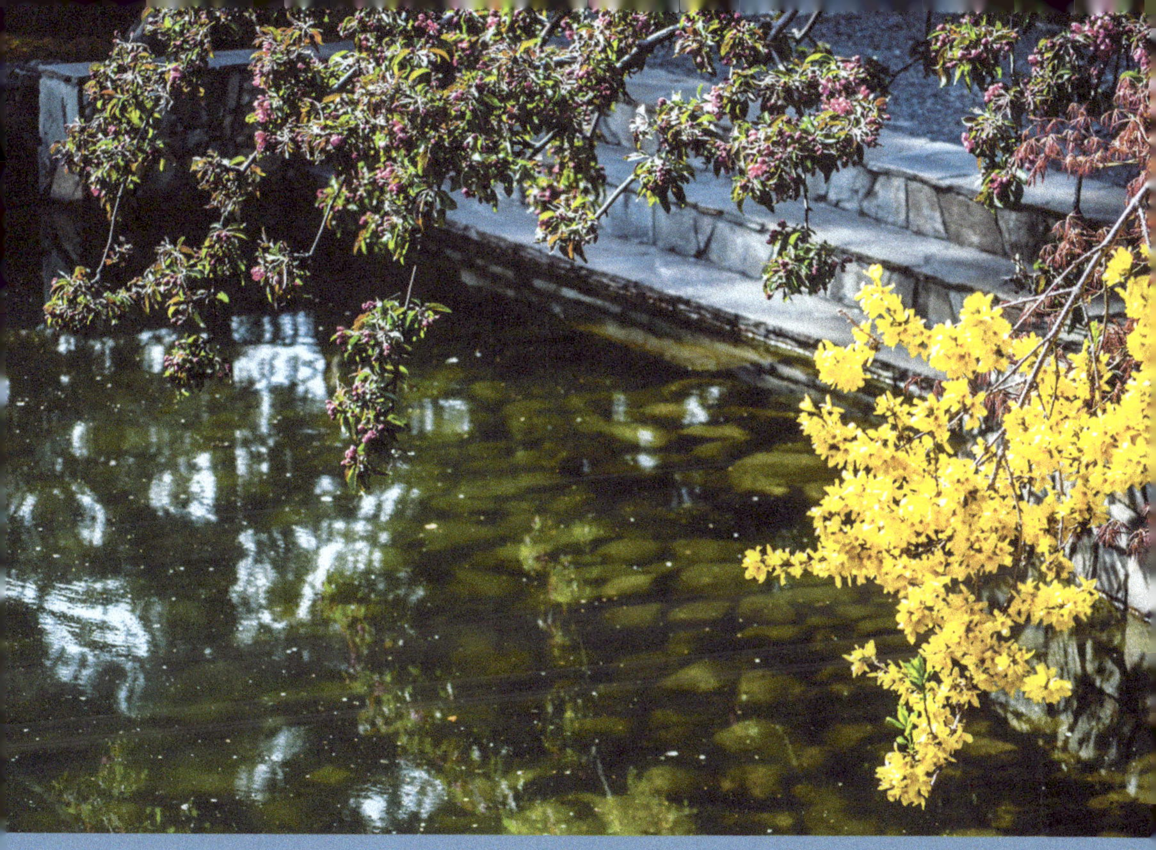

Crabapple and Forsythia swapped jokes whenever the garden was empty. When people walked by, they fell silent. They knew visitors would be shocked by their ribald jokes.

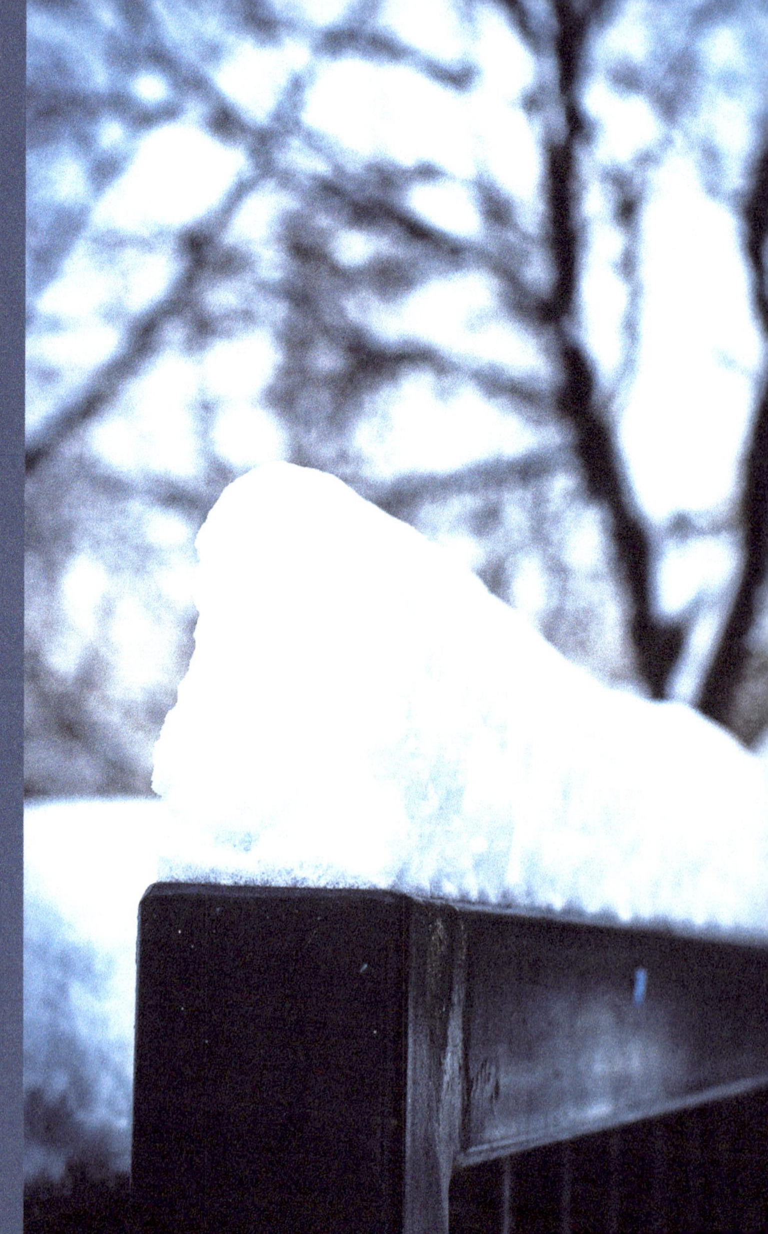

"Wooh-ooh-ooh!" Snow was a locomotive, pulling a load of freight. For some reason no one moved out of her way, though she was running full throttle.

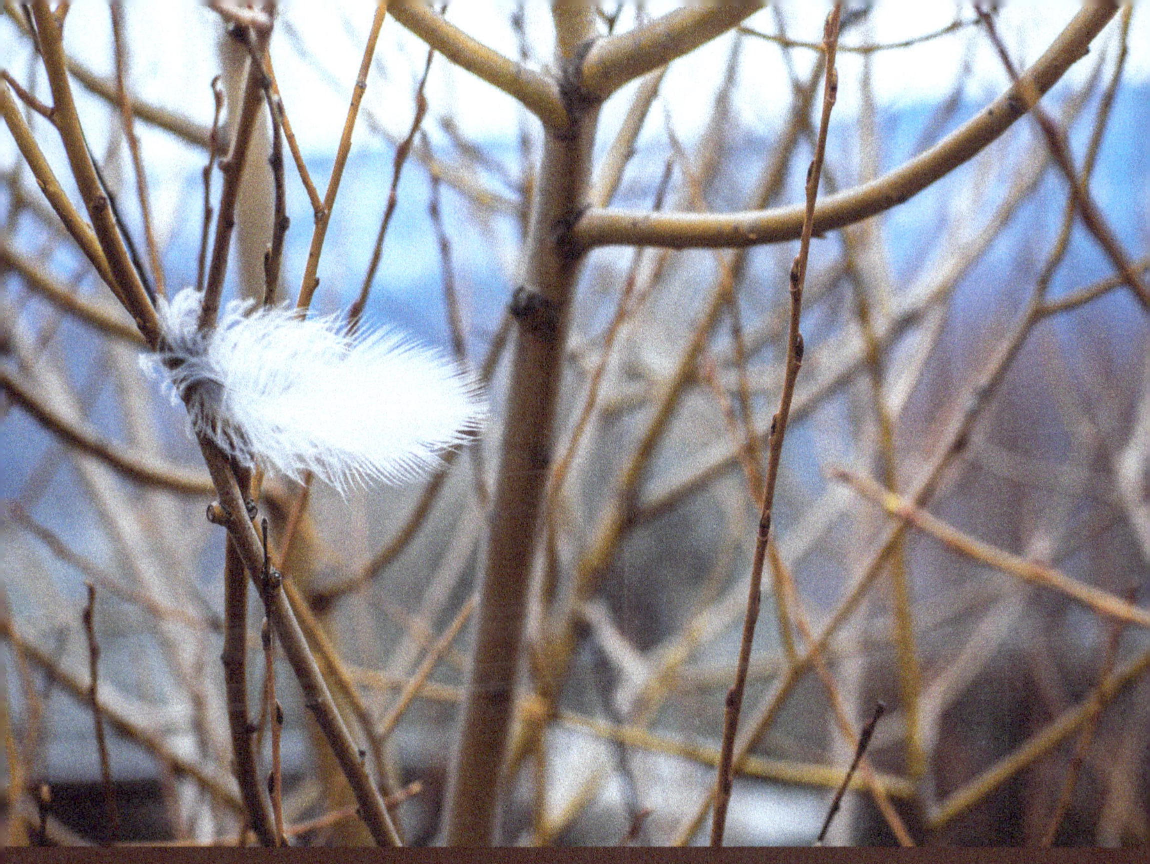

"Let me go," cried Feather. "I have more places to see." Willow, whose traveling days ended when he changed from seed to seedling, bargained with Feather. "Tell me about the world, and I'll shake you loose."

By day Deer
Woman
was a shy
watcher,
sheltered
within Tree.
But on
full-moon
nights, she
left her
hiding place
and danced
wildly
beneath the
stars.

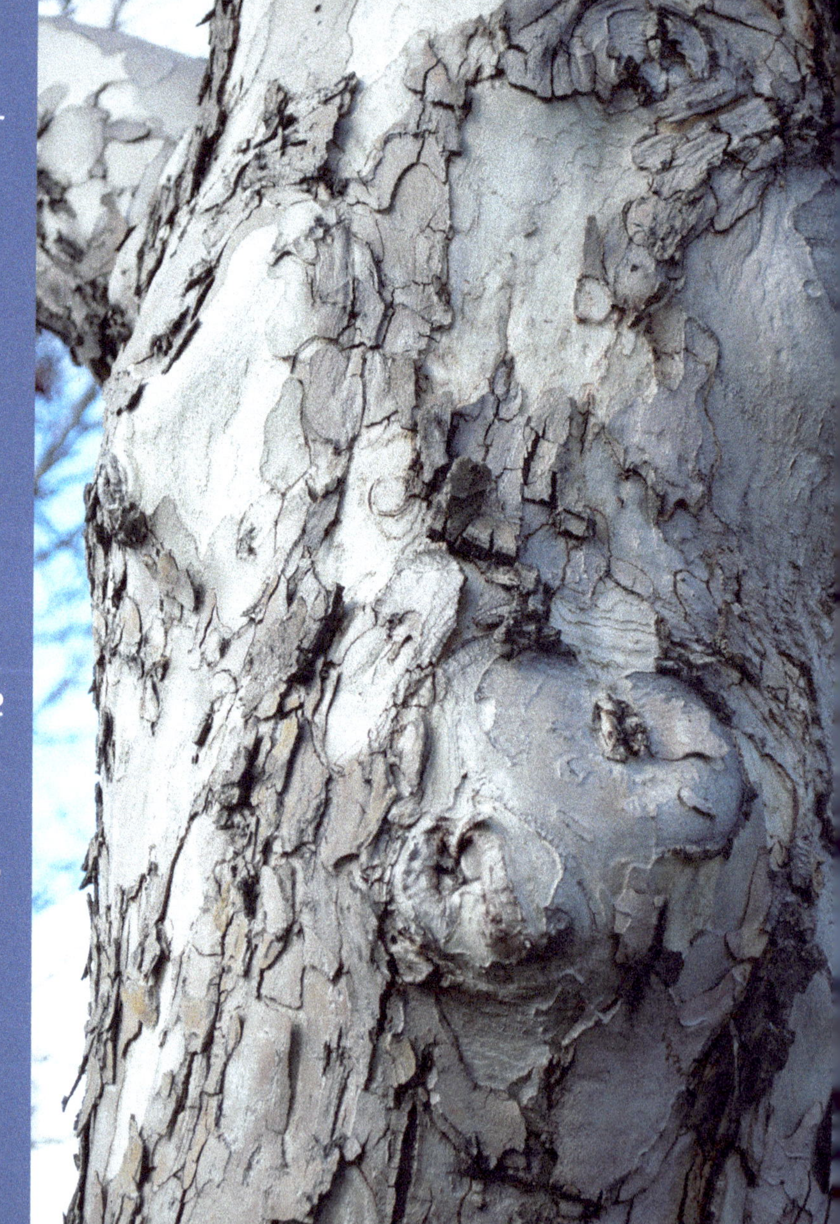

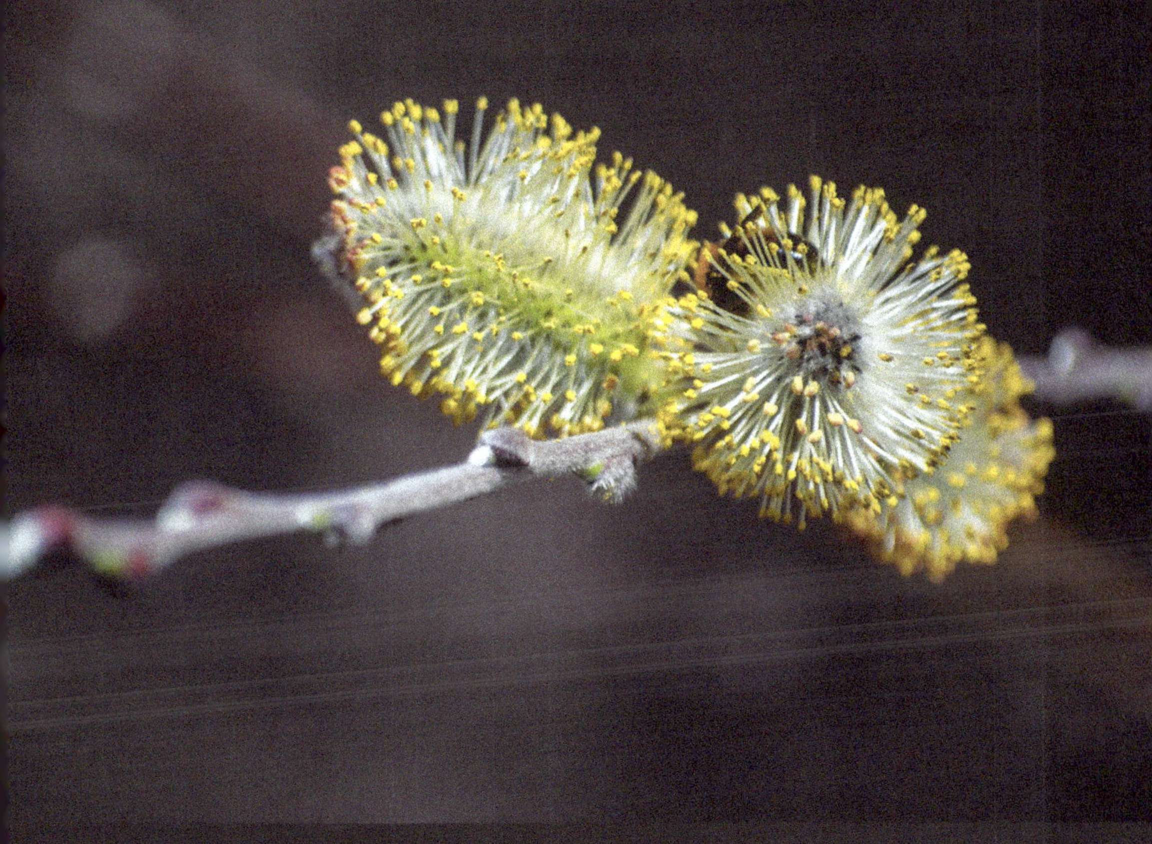

The First Blooms Race had barely been
announced when Pussy Willows jumped the
queue and took the lead.

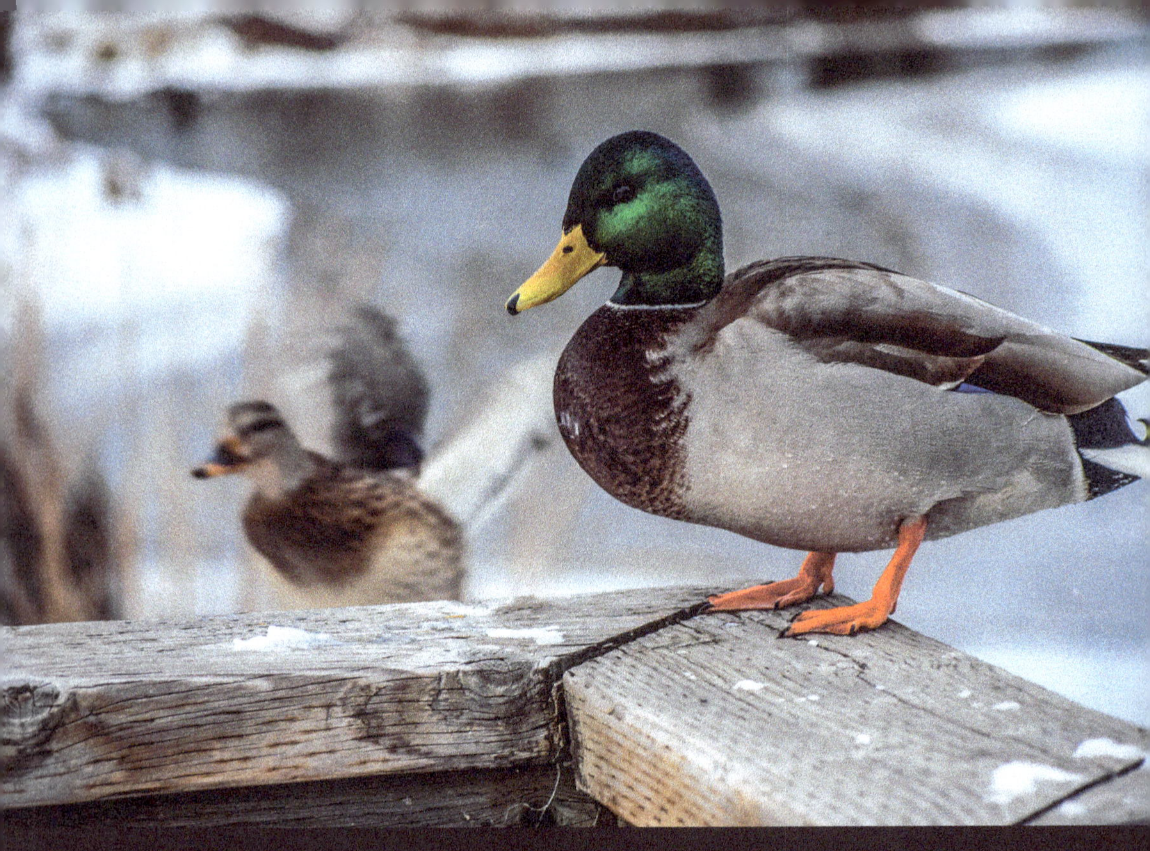

"Hey, sweetheart, hand over the seed before Greedy Girl lands." Mallard was frustrated. He tried so hard to speak Human, but they were truly language impaired.

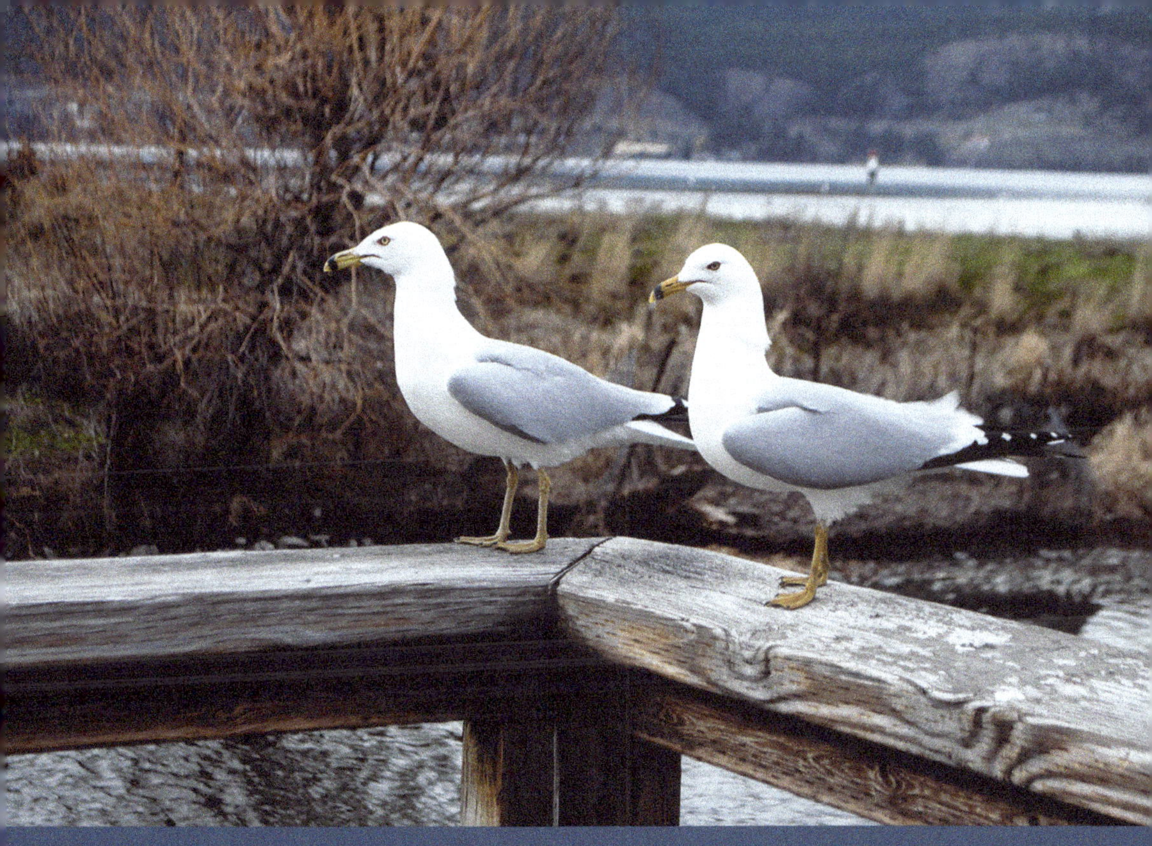

The twins checked out the marsh. Rumor had it some party birds had moved in, with strange ways that might liven things up for everyone.

She pulled on
her tutu,
brushed her
hair, and
began to sing
and dance.
She
performed
with such
abandon her
costume and
hair floated
away. Birds
came from
miles around
to watch in
amazement.

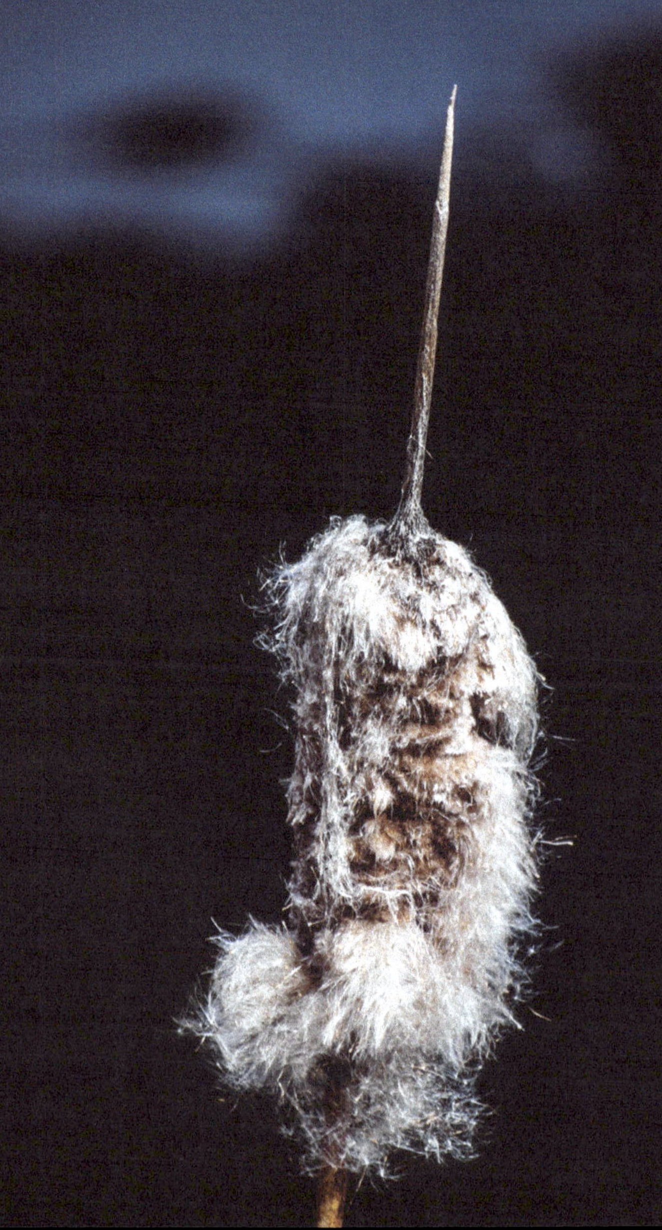

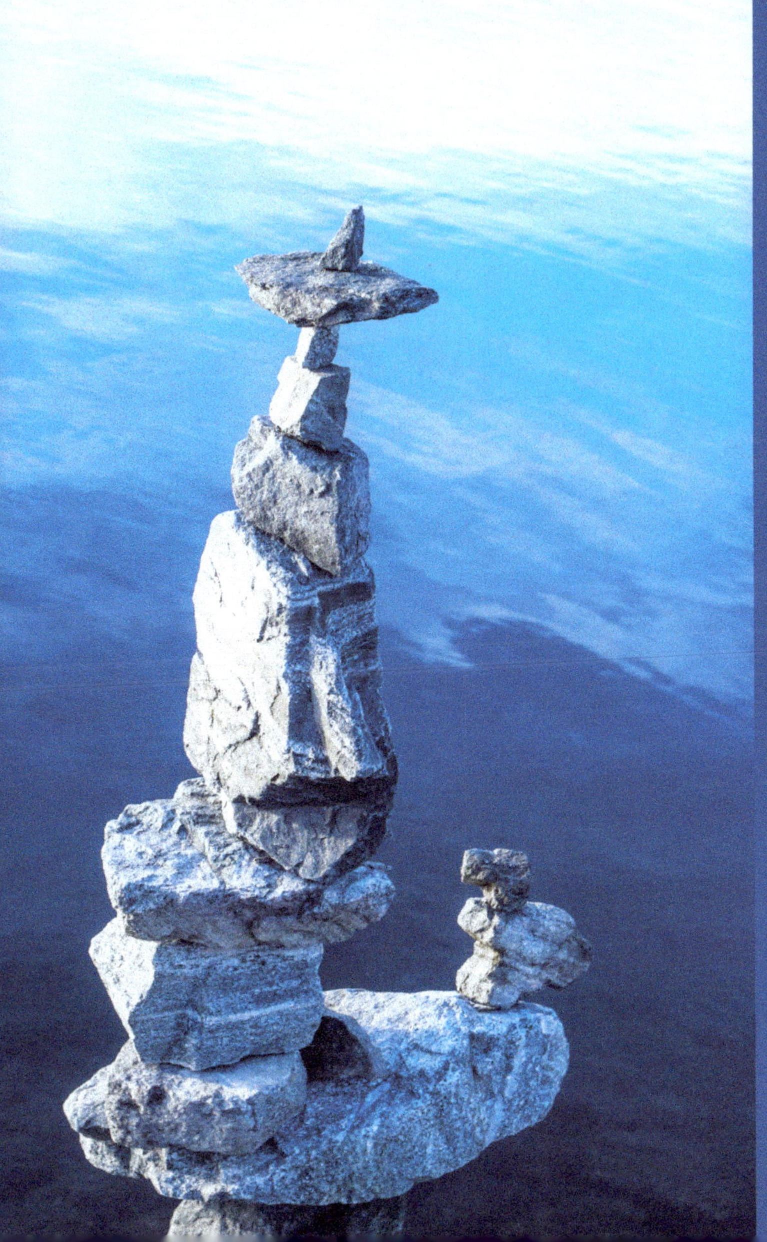

Arms akimbo, hat in place, Tall-Guy Inukshuk felt himself fill with stories. He looked down at attentive Dog Pile below and began, "Once upon a time…"

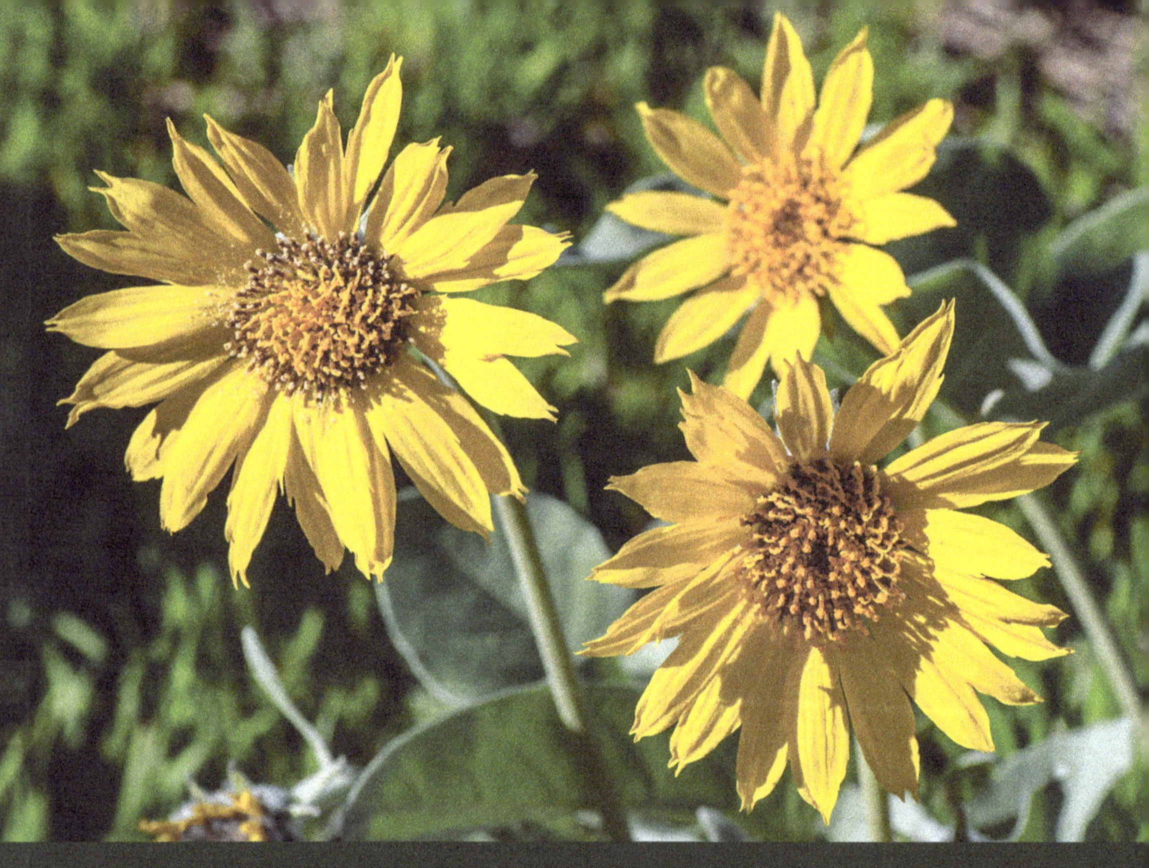

The others were harmonizing with the wind. Shy Flower plucked up her courage. Today she would sing in the key of free, no matter how many times they told her to "just wave the words."

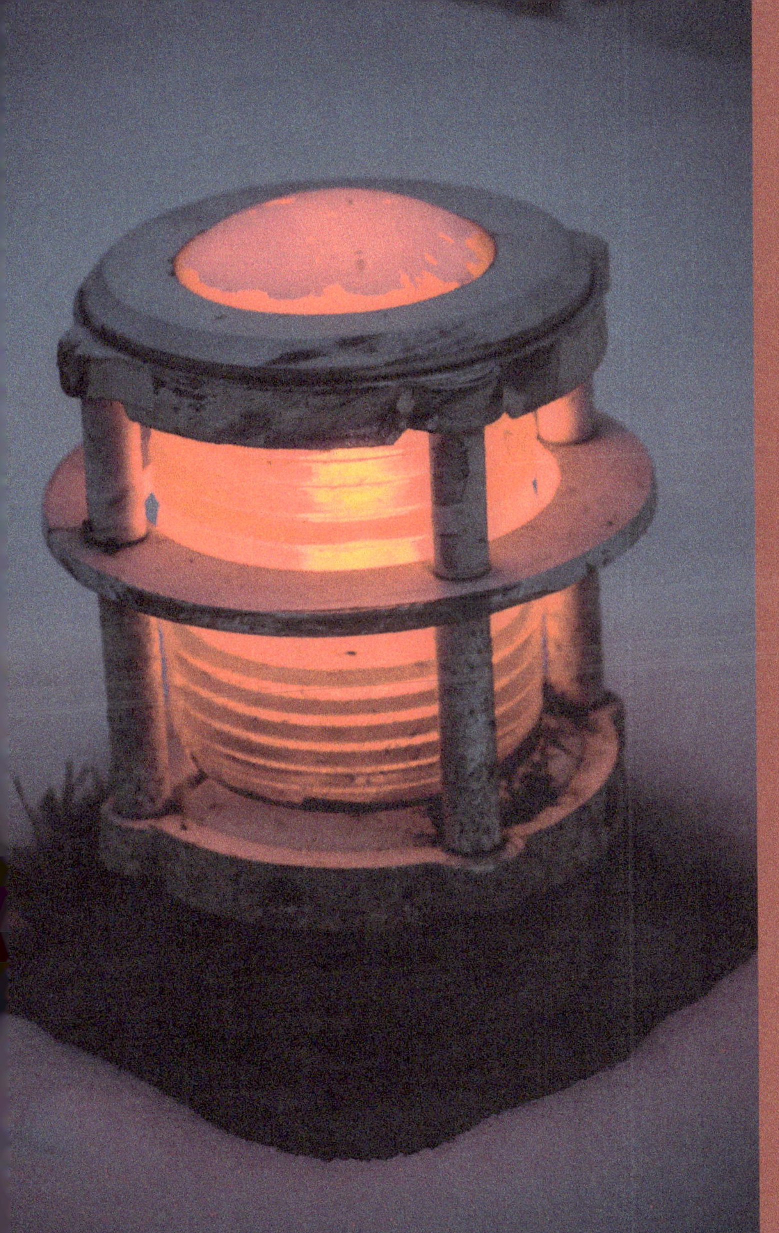

Lantern loved his red glow. He hoped this year the city workers would forget to change his bulb back to white after Christmas.

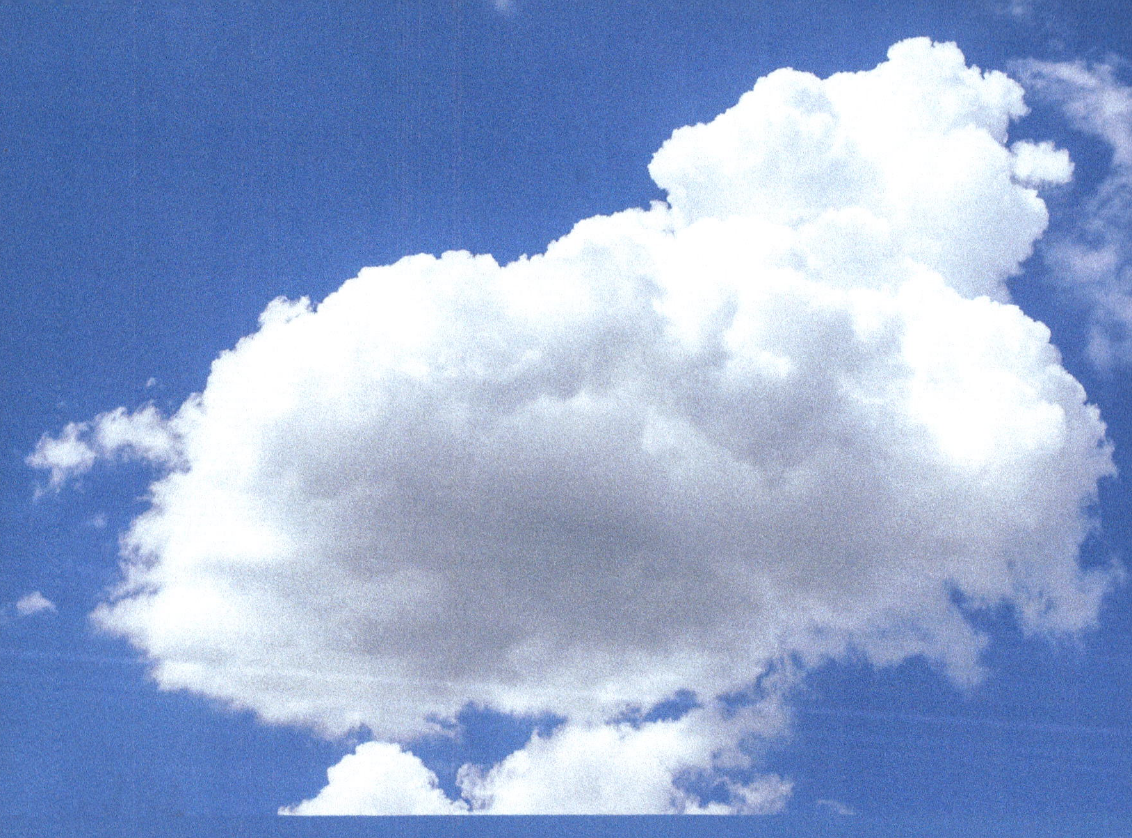

Today she was Charlotte, chubby cheeked and curly haired. When she couldn't get the nose to stick to her face, she lost interest. She made a fluffy cushion and took a nap instead.

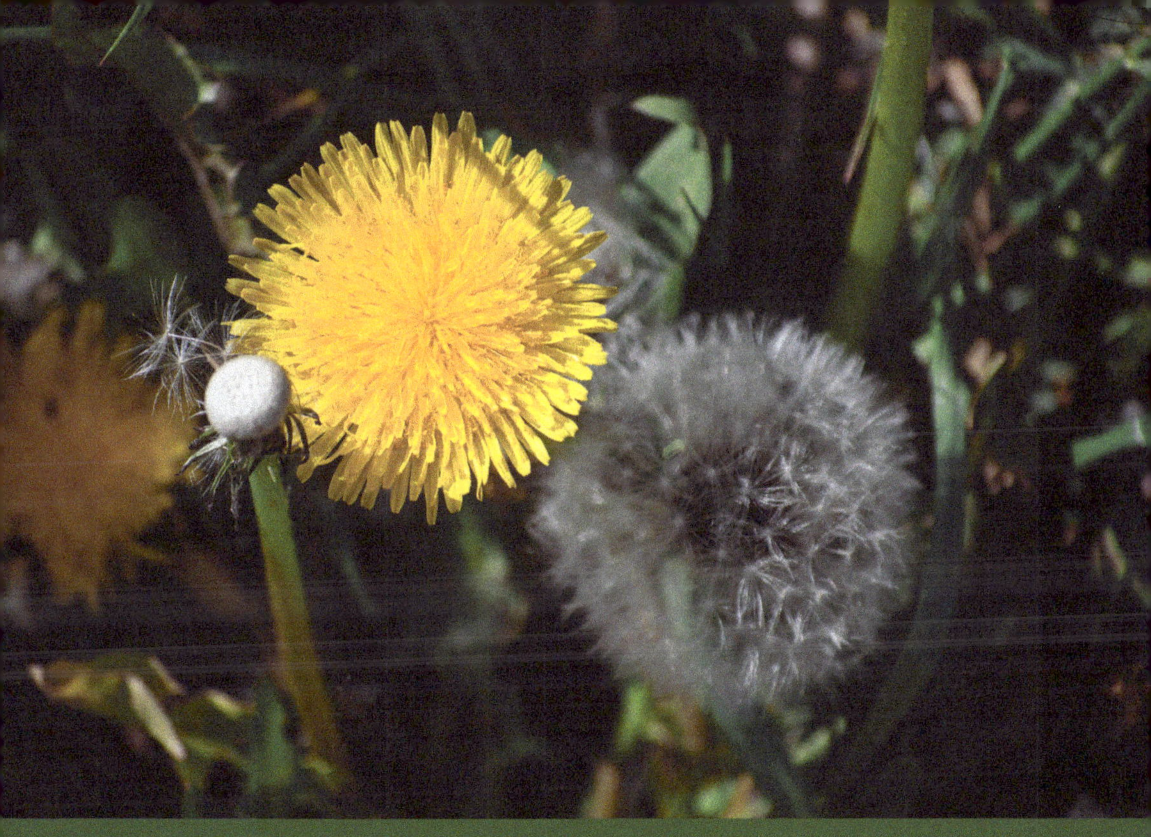

Her friends became seeds and floated away.
Young Dandelion was sorry to see them go but
excited by what lay ahead. "Farewell," they
shouted. "We're off to see the world and start
families of our own."

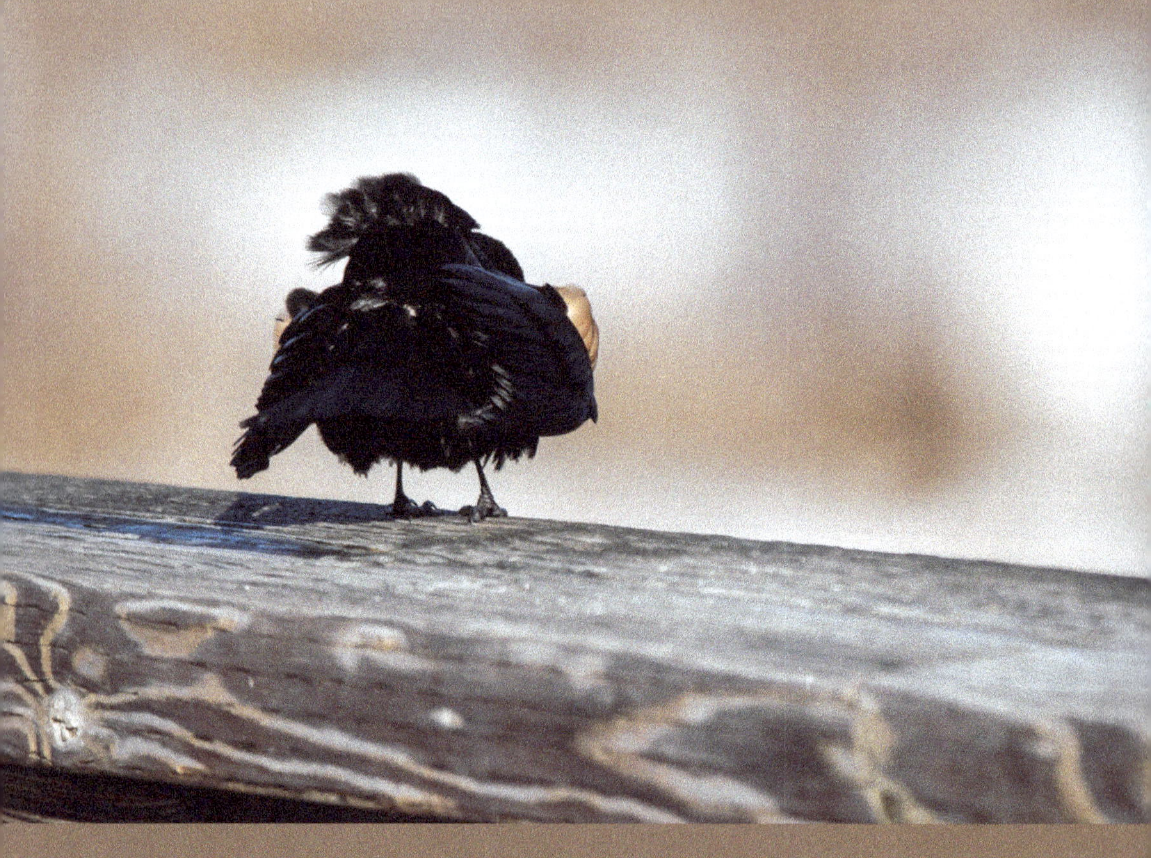

"Back off, Wind. I'm trying to impress the ladies. You're messing up my feathers and making me look clumsy."

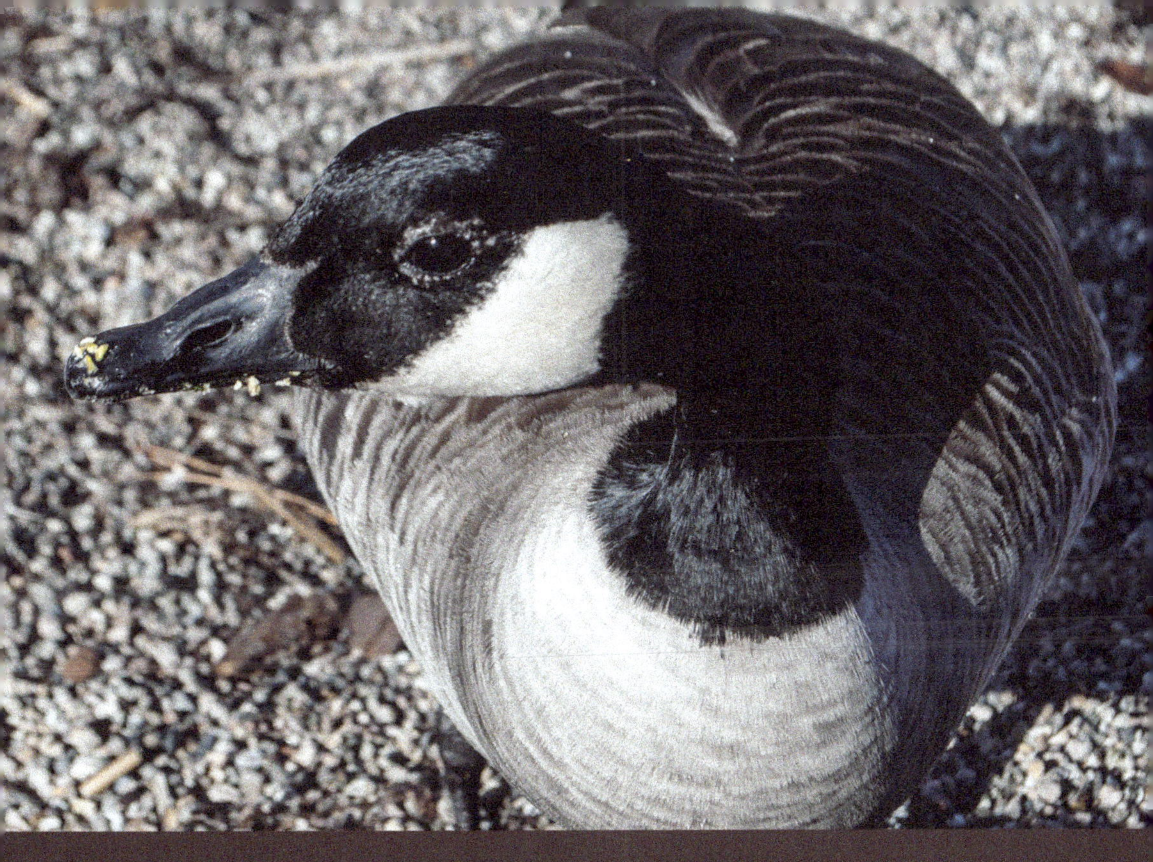

The eggs were laid. Her mate was guarding them. She was free to forage for food. She was new to motherhood and wondered how her life would change when the eggs cracked open.

People laughed and said he looked like ET, yearning for home. They did not comprehend the thrill of standing firm while Bay of Fundy tides rushed around his neck. His life was full of adventure.

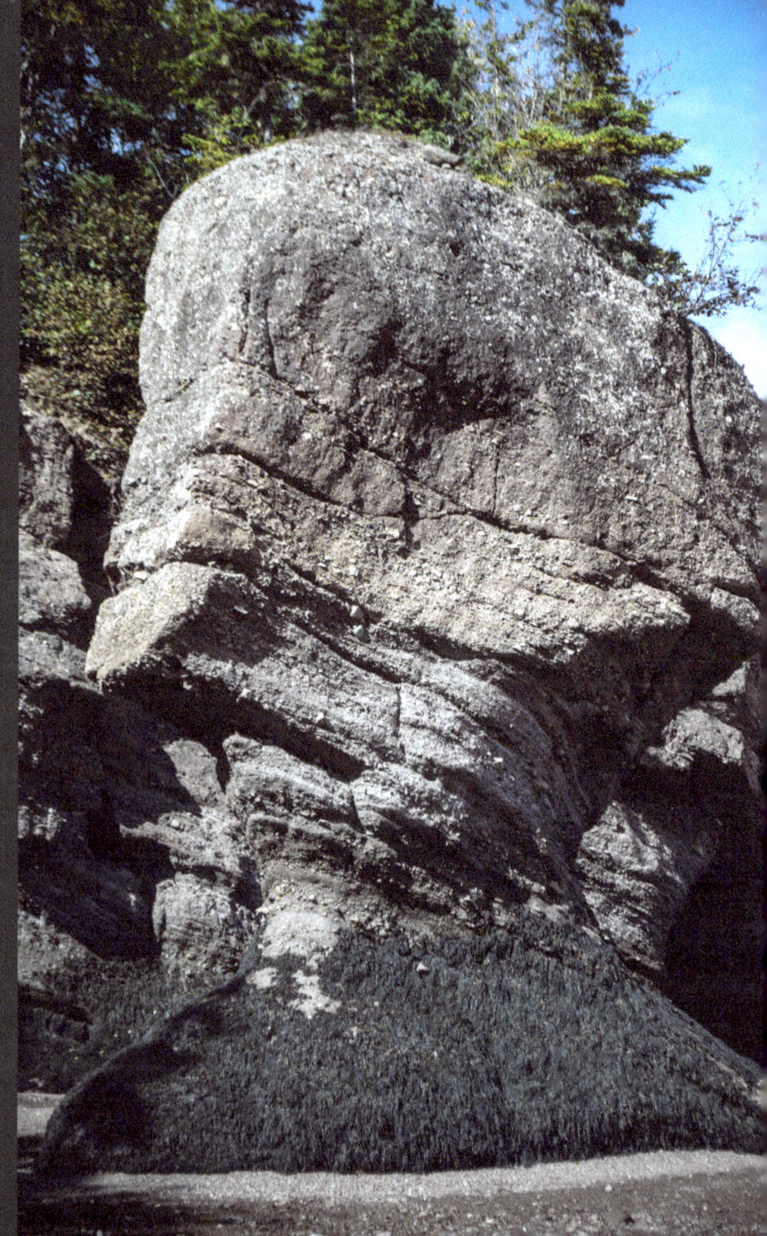

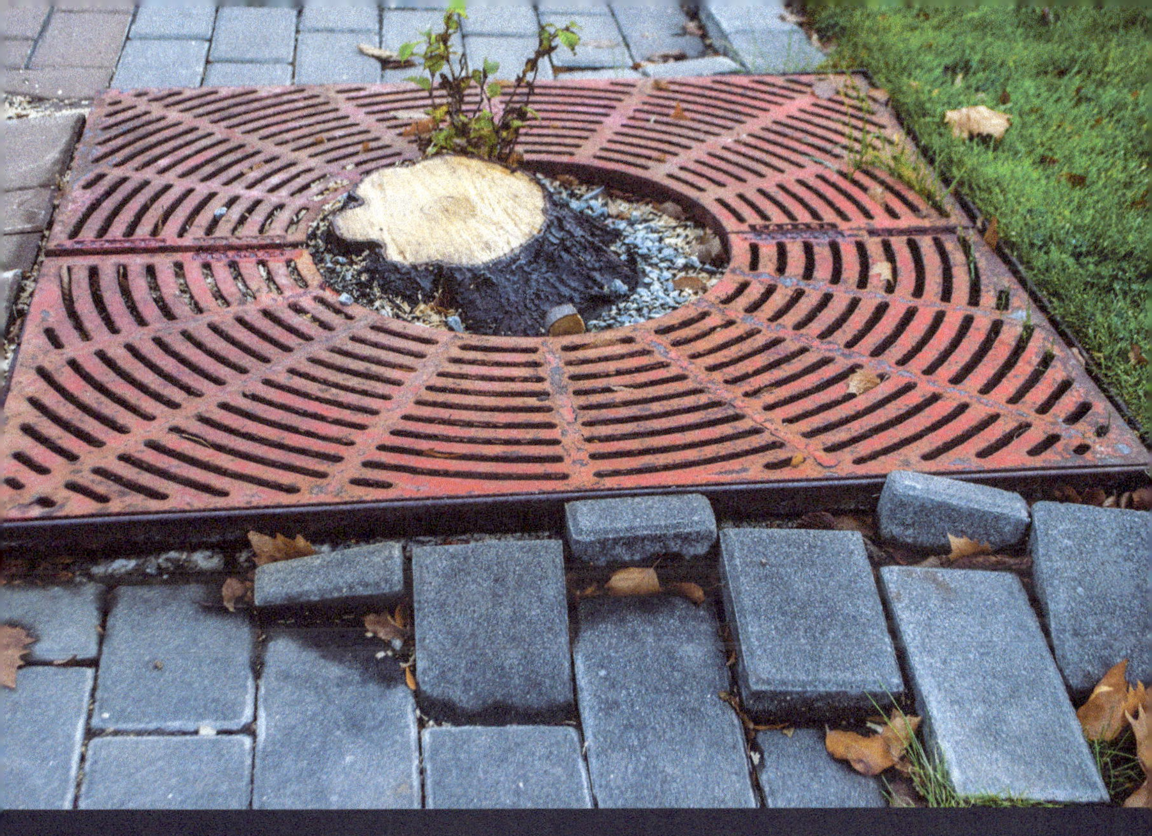

Tree pushed up the bricks smothering her roots.
Ah, it felt good to breathe more freely.
Unfortunately, groundskeepers were not
impressed with her initiative and took a power
saw to her.

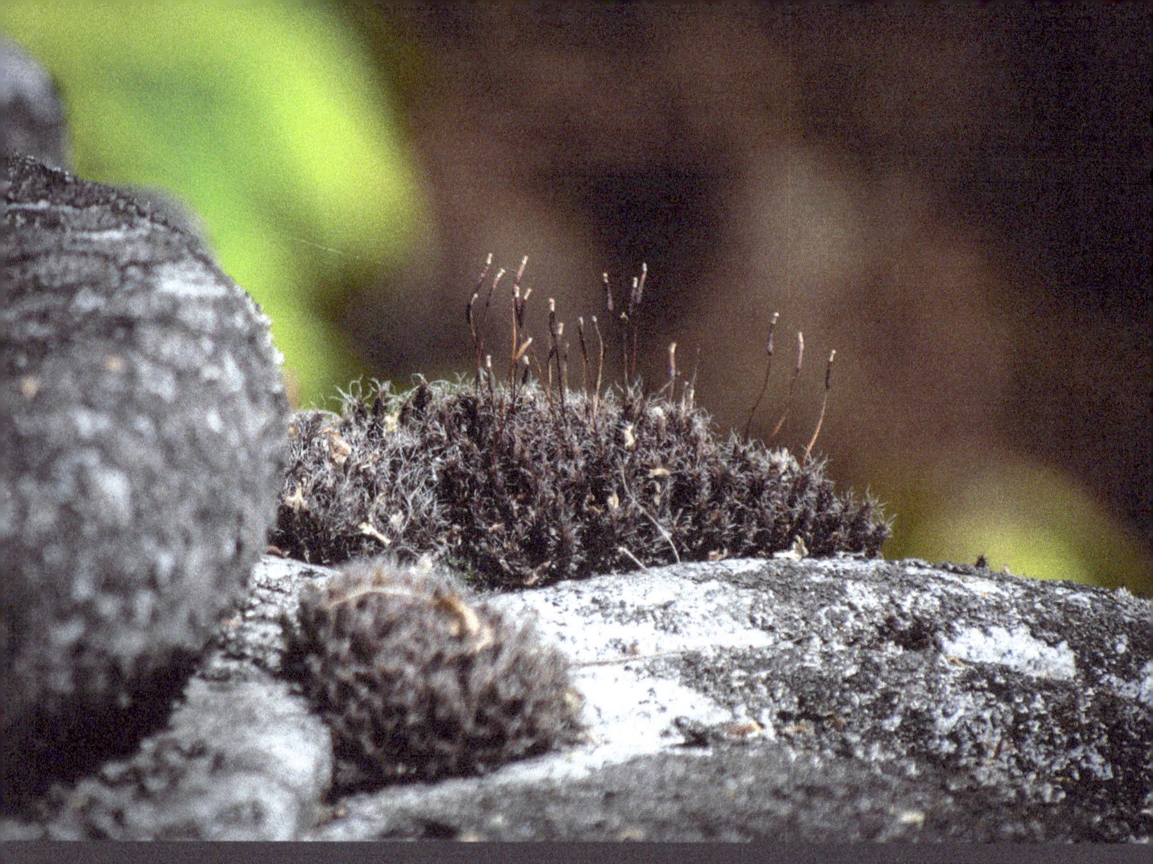

Visitors saw only some bits of moss growing on
a sculpture. But to the spider who spun a
delicate web between moss and stone, it was the
whole, glorious world.

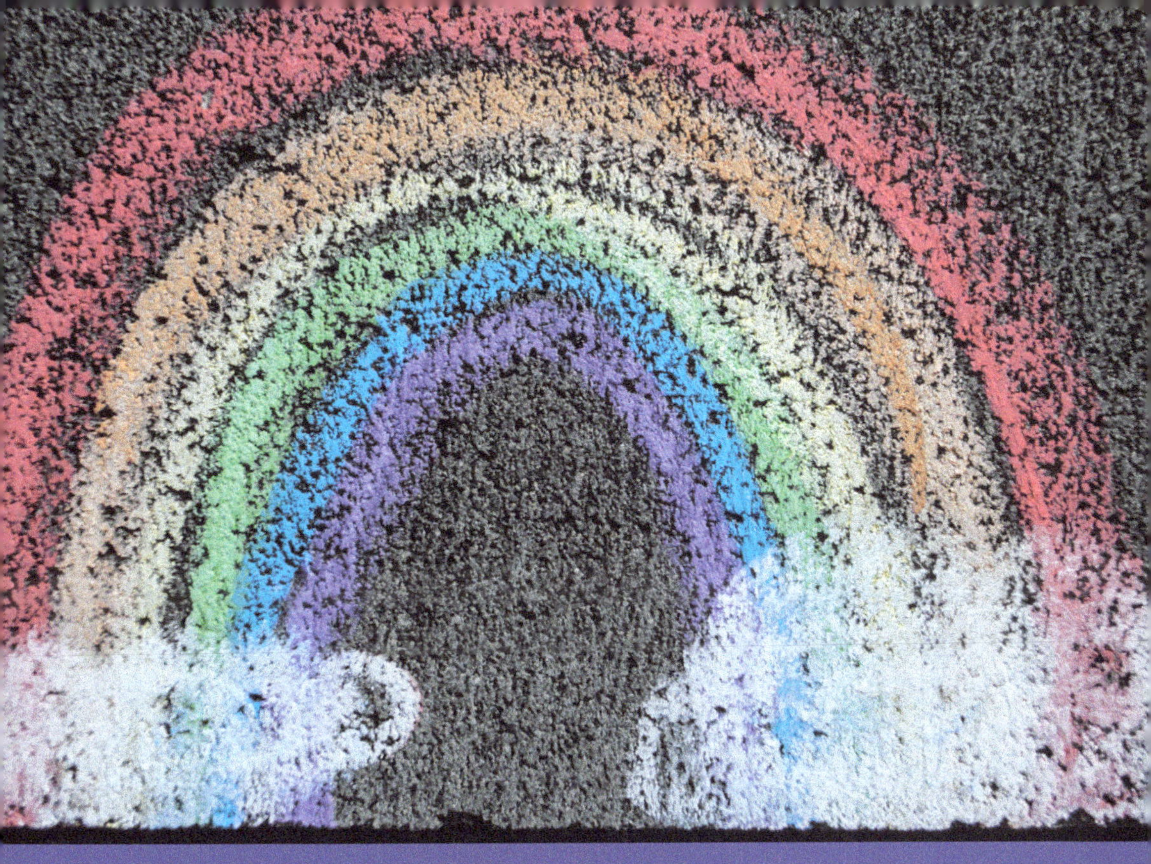

Grownups walked over the chalk drawing without a glance. Children knew rainbow stripes were magical. They stopped and made a wish, sure it would come true.

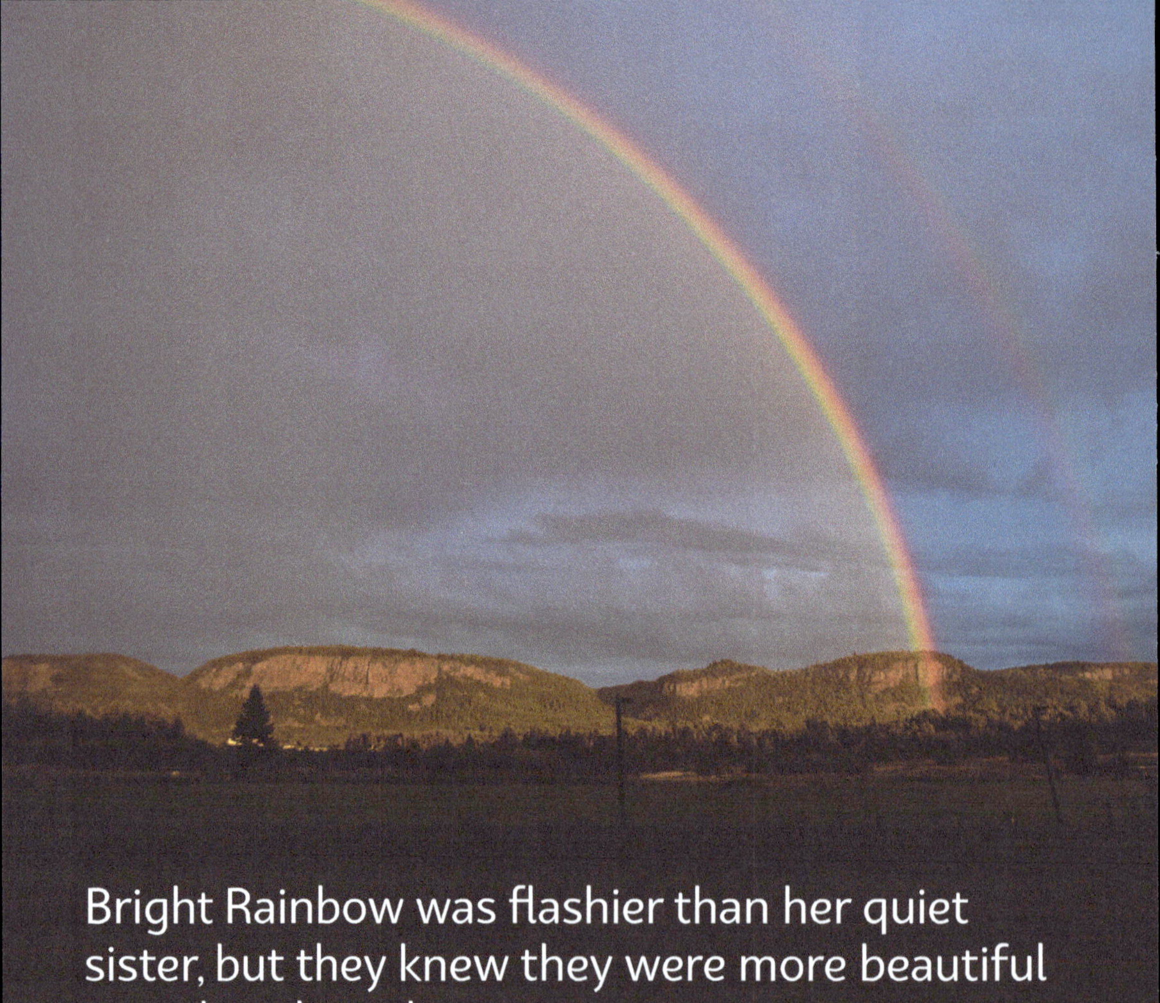

Bright Rainbow was flashier than her quiet sister, but they knew they were more beautiful together than alone.

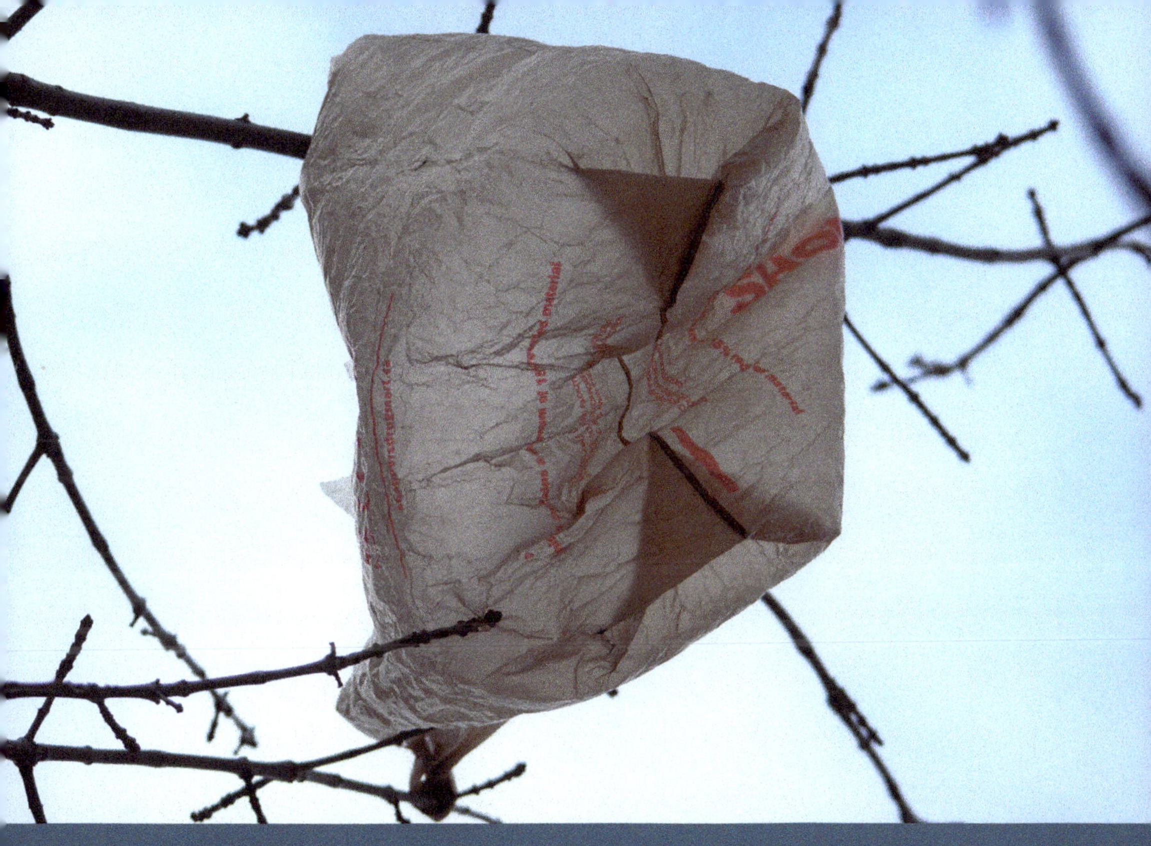

Bag heard the humans say they were going to use him for garbage. "I'll show them," he said. Wind helped him fly free. Tree gave him safe landing. "You can't catch me now," he laughed at the people below.

~ 27 ~

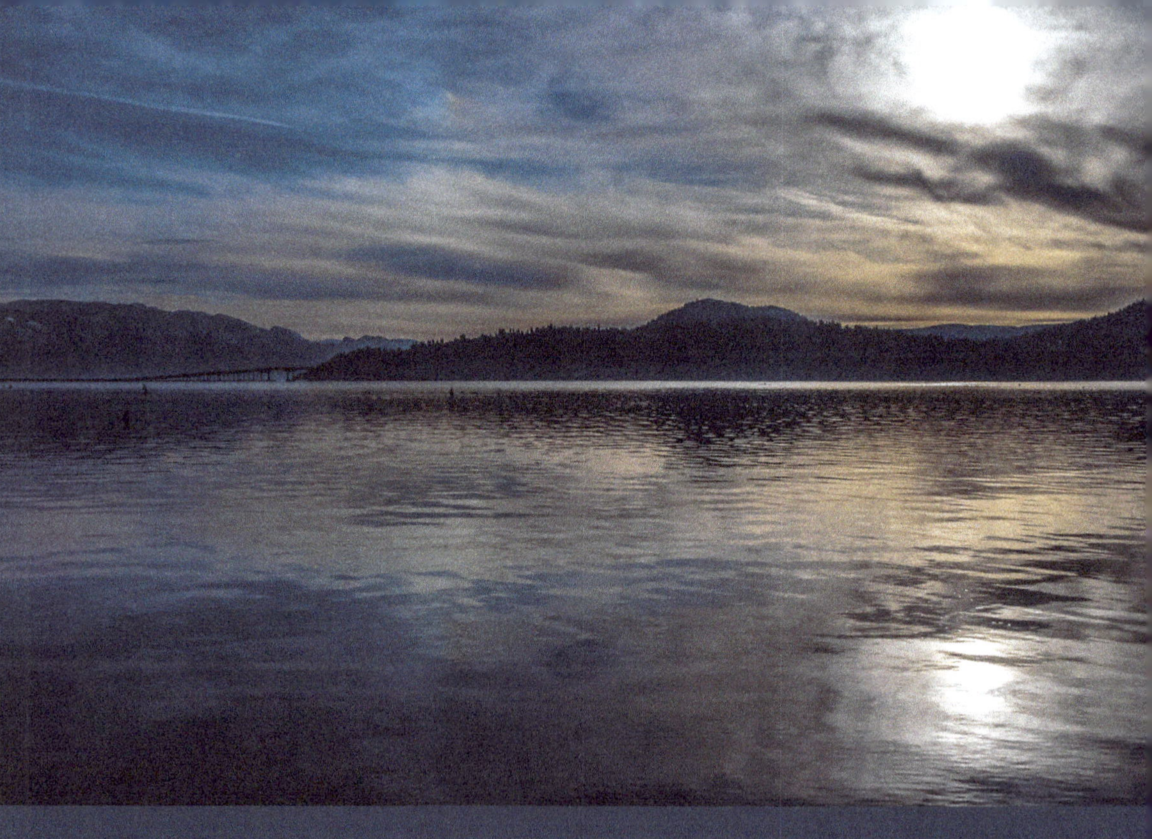

Clouds and water poured their best artistic talents into creating a stunning scene for the people out walking. Their results were fleeting, which made them all the more precious.

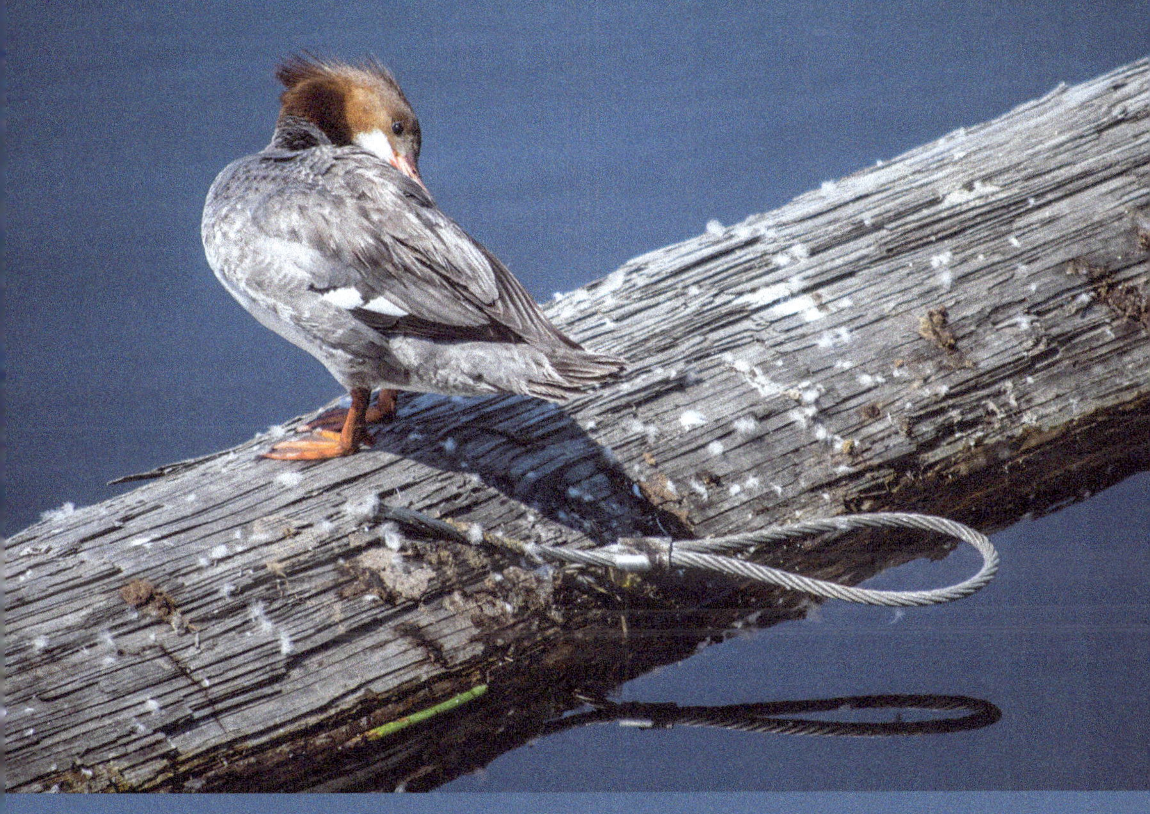

"A noose. I'm sure that's a noose." Merganser was an educated bird, schooled in strange, human ways. Still, he could not fathom such a bizarre concept. He soon lost interest and focused on something much more interesting: females.

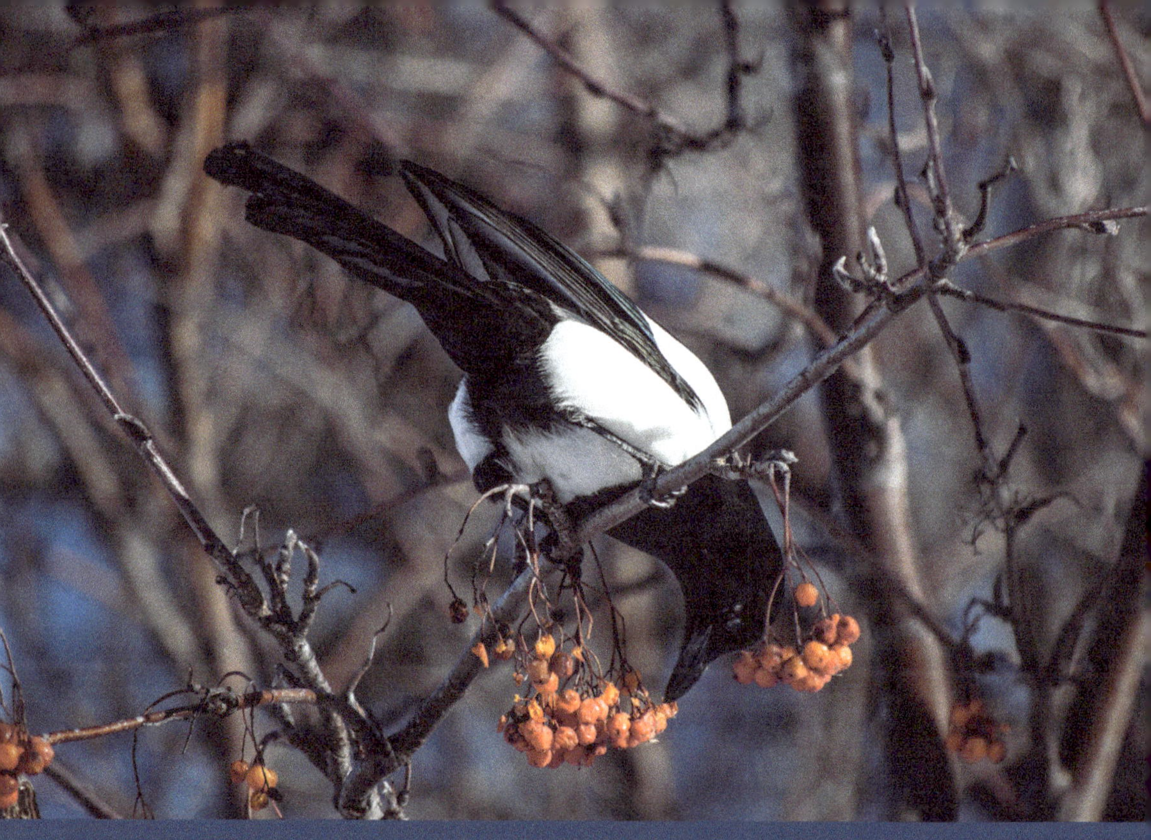

Magpie leaned precariously, determined to eat every last berry. "Tree," he complained, "I want you to grow berries above the branch. I get dizzy trying to reach them."

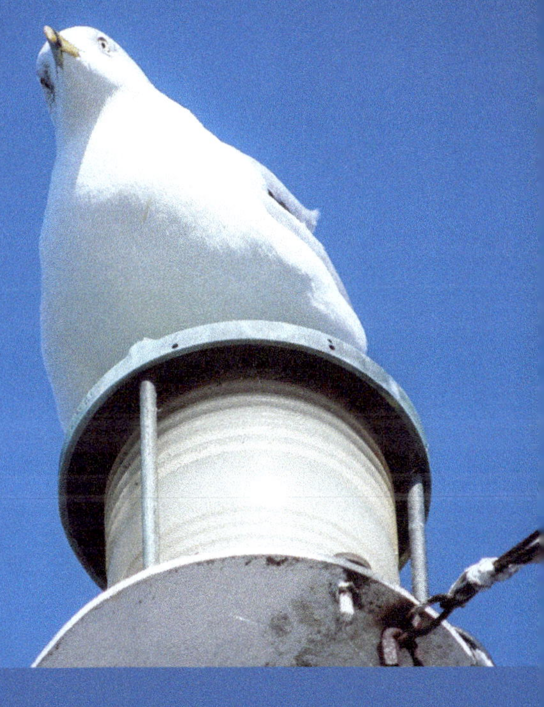

Seagull looked peaceful and innocent to passersby. They did not know he was watching for someone with a bald head to pass below. He had plans that were definitely not innocent.

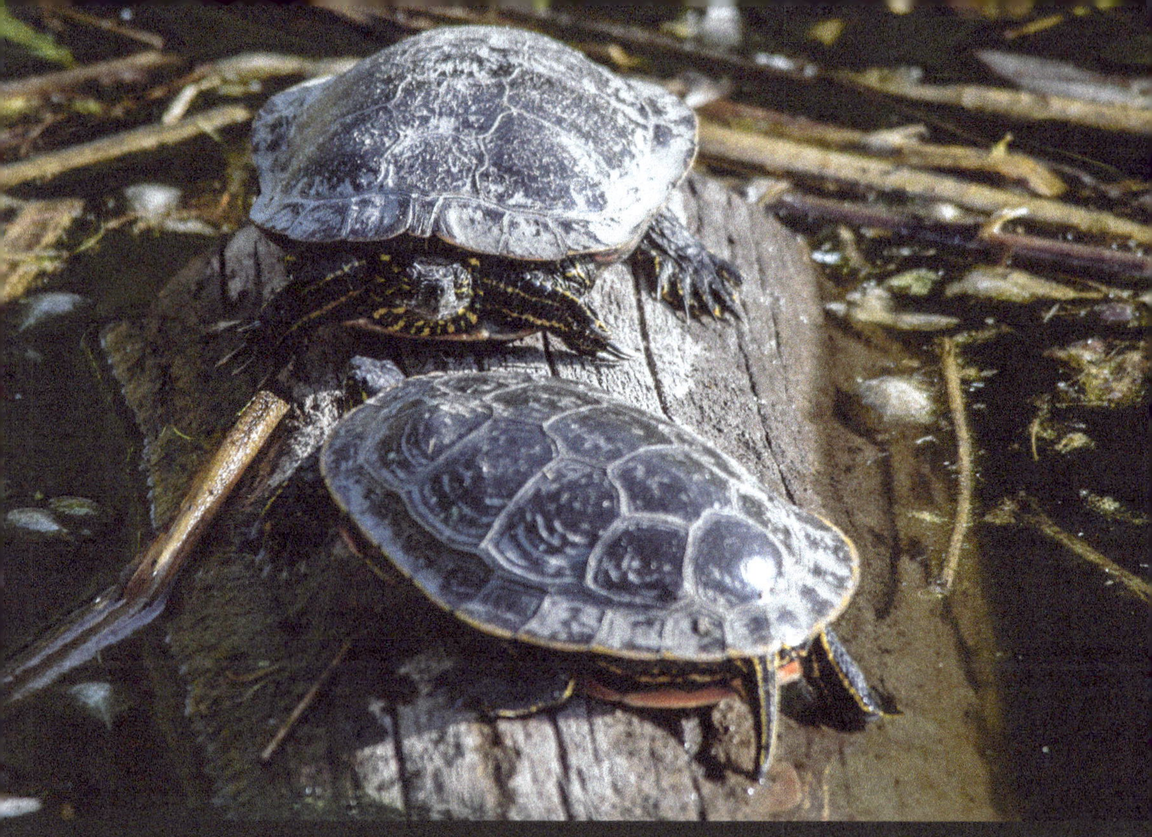

The two friends met frequently on their favorite log. Mostly they sat in silence, enjoying each other's company. On rare occasions they shared a conversation of a word or two.

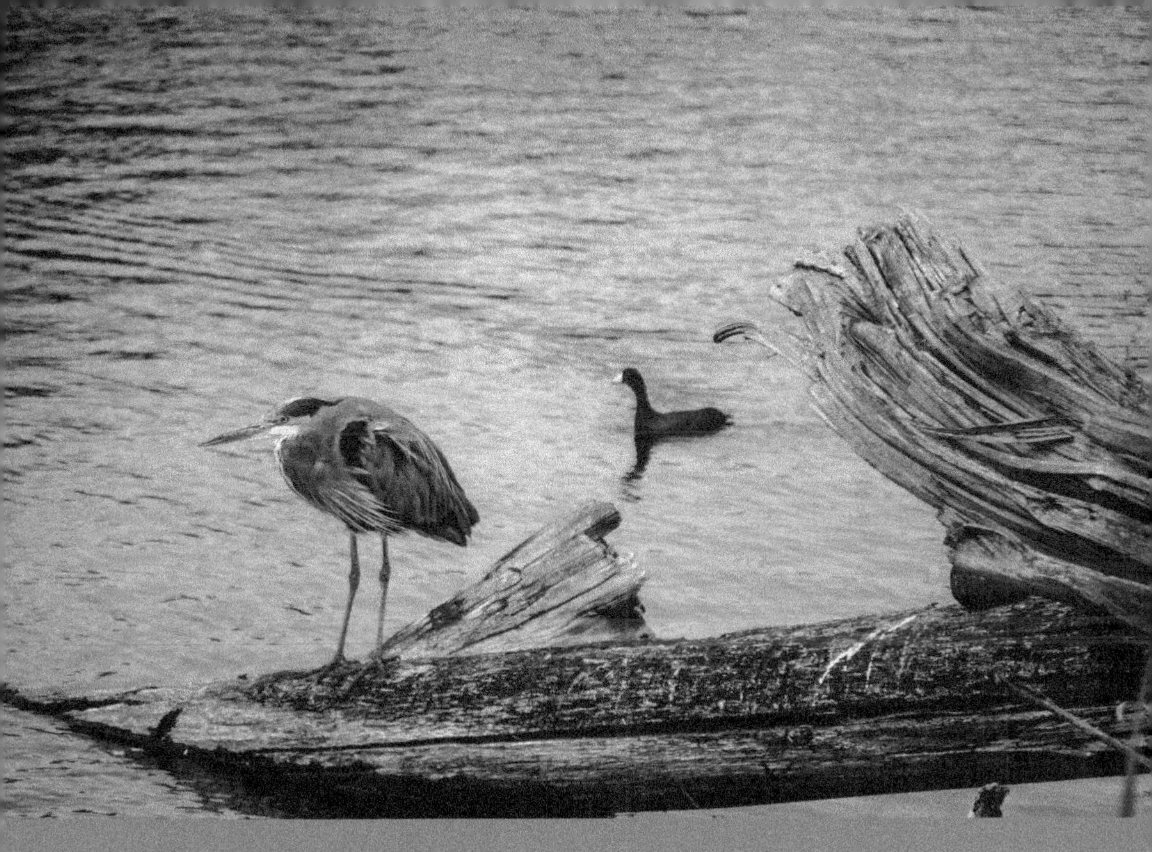

"Hey, Heron! Whatcha doing? Seen any fish?" Great Blue Heron sighed. If Coot did not move on soon, he would scare away the fishy lunch swimming by.

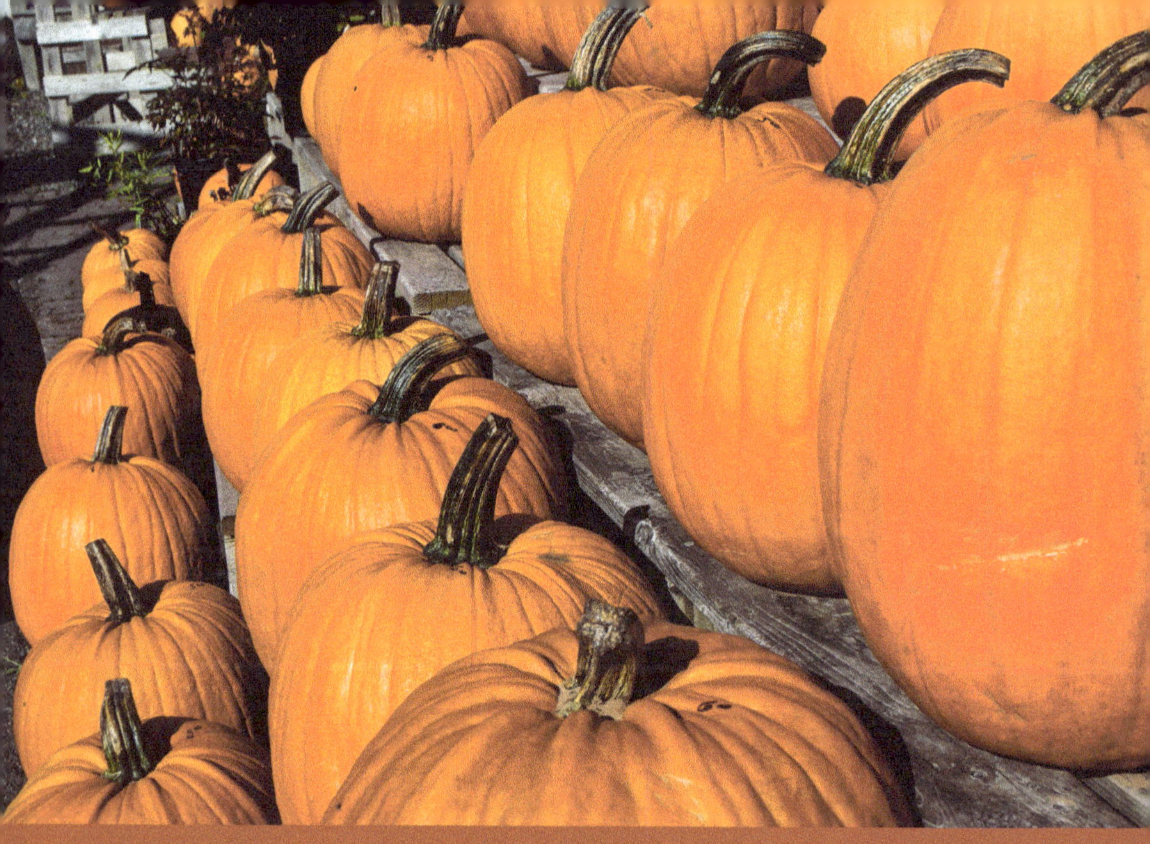

The pumpkin choir practiced scales in preparation for their annual concert. It was so hard to learn all the songs when members kept disappearing.

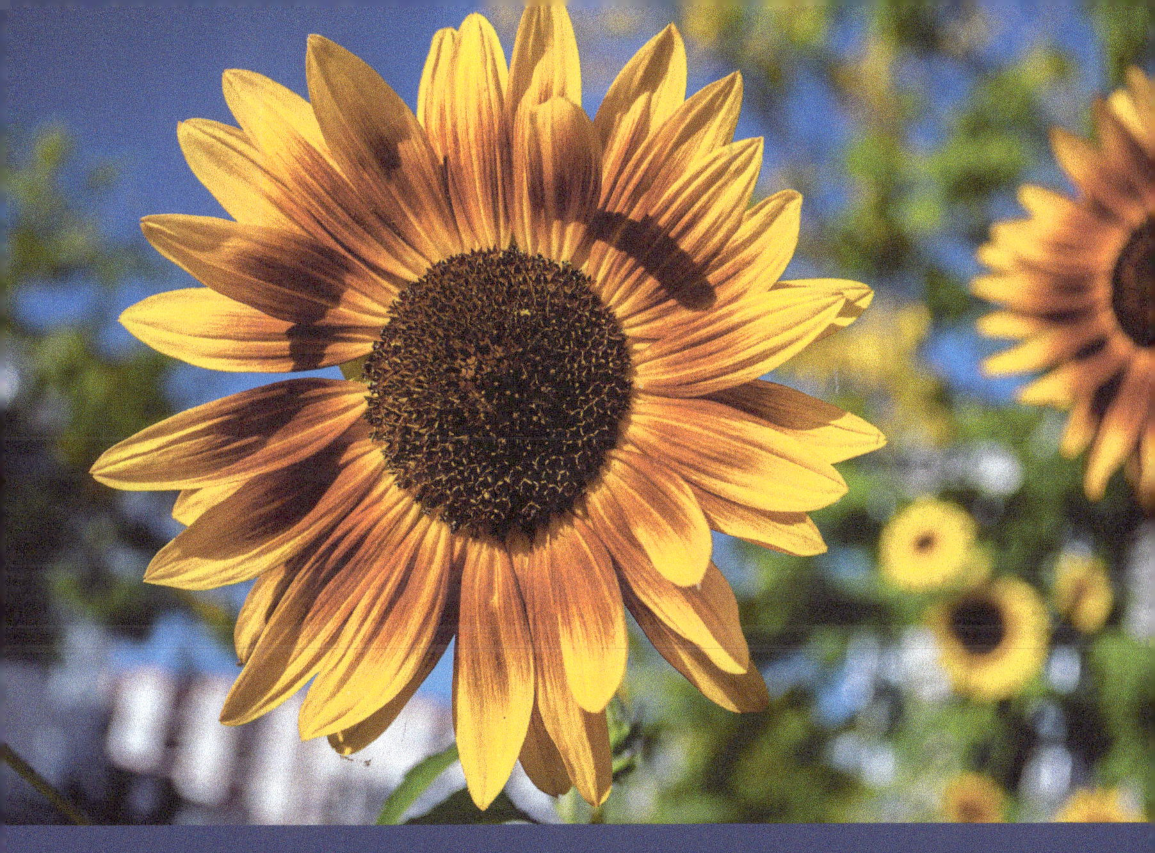

She stepped forward, cleared her throat, and surprised the audience. They expected opera or, at the very least, roots and blues. Instead, she nodded in the wind and rapped scandalously and uproariously.   ~ 35 ~

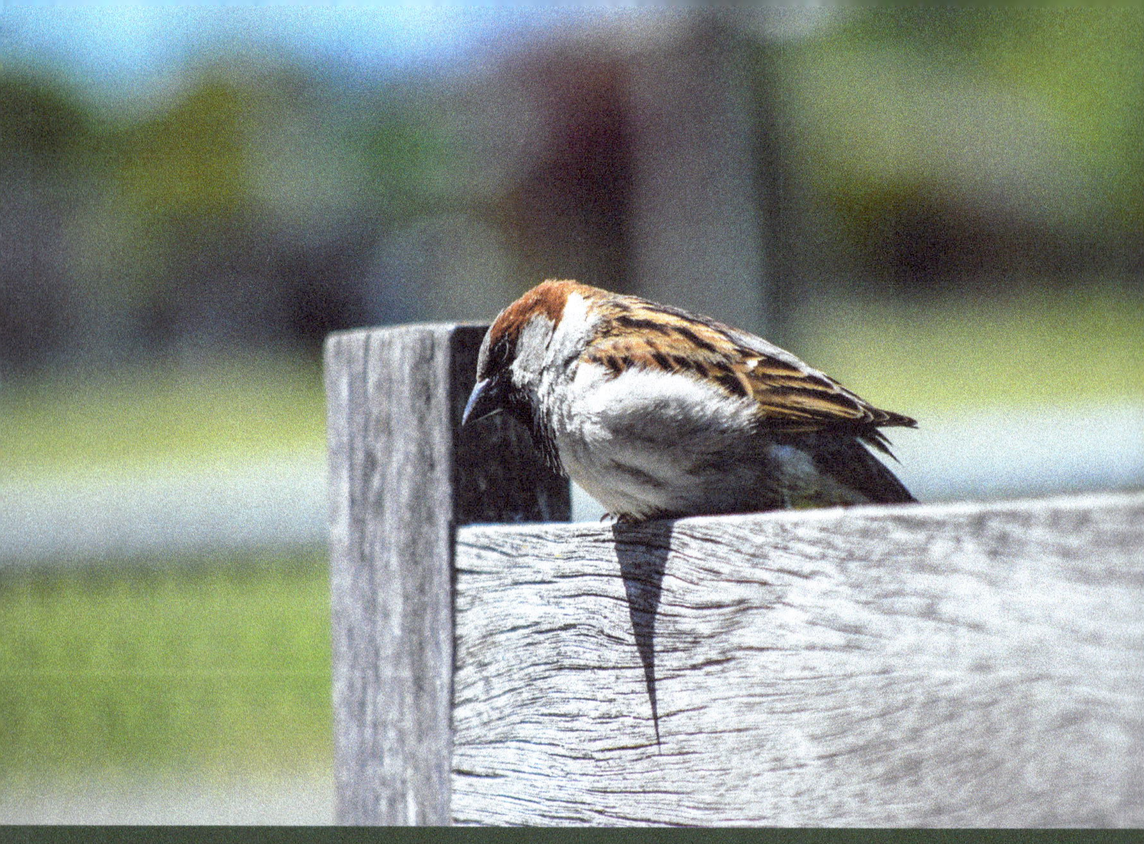

Sparrow looked sleepy, but he was planning his attack on the piece of apple below. Unfortunately, by the time he worked out the clever logistics, Squirrel had devoured the prize.

ABOUT THE AUTHOR

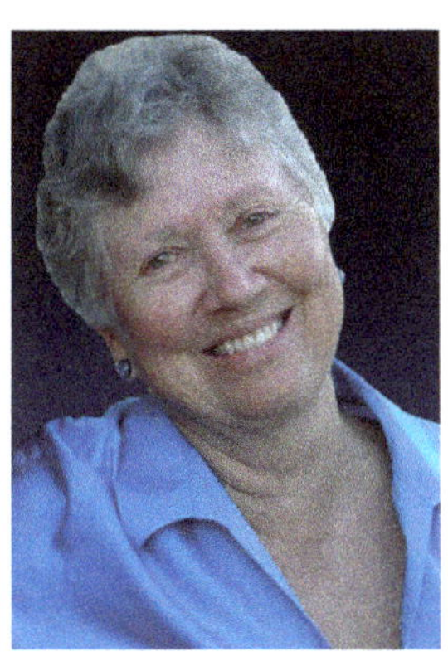

Cathryn Wellner is a writer, photographer and storyteller living in Kelowna, British Columbia, Canada.

Recent books by Cathryn include:
Parts of Me Are Still Amazing
That Tree Talked to Me
Hope Wins
Feisty Aging
In the Hug of Hills
Millie's Feathered Foster Family
Turkey Baby and the Hungry Hawk
Turkey Baby Finds Her Magic

You can find links to these and her other books at cathrynwellner.com. Contact her at cathryn@cathrynwellner.com or 778-478-2760. Her photographs can be found on her Web site, as well as on Facebook and Instagram.

BE A BOOK REVIEW ANGEL

If you enjoyed this book, please post a review on Amazon or Goodreads. Share it with friends and rave about it on social media. You can contact the author at cathryn@cathrynwellner.com.

Authors rely on their readers to help spread the word about books they like. People who review books are special kinds of reader angels. I guarantee when you review this book, or any other book that has given you pleasure in any way, you'll feel those wings poking out your back. Look closely in the mirror, and you might even see a halo.

Credits

Fonts used on cover and design pages: Saltash, BasicSans, Salt & Pepper. Font used in stories: Bw Surco. Logo font: Ed's Market. All fonts, plus the film edges and texture on the cover are licensed through DesignCuts.

The beautiful blue wings on the dedication page were created by the amazing foxeysquirrel. The book was designed in PhotoShop.

Thank you to the creative people who designed the unique fonts and elements incorporated in this book. I continually learn from you.

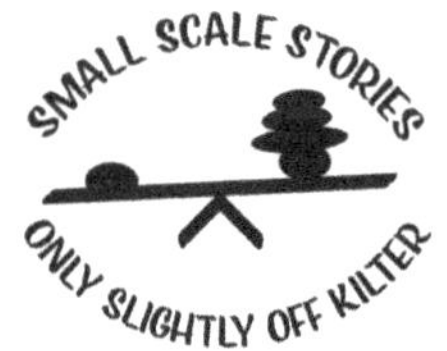